A BATTLE OF BRITAIN SPITFIRE SQUADRON

THE MEN AND MACHINES OF 152 SQUADRON IN THE SUMMER OF 1940

A BATTLE OF BRITAIN SPITFIRE SQUADRON

THE MEN AND MACHINES OF 152 SQUADRON IN THE SUMMER OF 1940

DANNY BURT

Frontline Books

A BATTLE OF BRITAIN SPITFIRE SQUADRON
The Men and Machines of 152 Squadron in the Summer of 1940

First published in Great Britain in 2018 by Frontline Books,
an imprint of Pen & Sword Books Ltd, Yorkshire - Philadelphia

Typeset in 10/13.5 Palatino Printed and bound by TJ International Ltd
Padstow, Cornwall

Pen & Sword Books Ltd incorporates the imprints of Pen & Sword Archaeology,
Atlas, Aviation, Battleground, Discovery, Family History, History, Maritime,
Military, Naval, Politics, Social History, Transport, True Crime, Claymore Press,
Frontline Books, Praetorian Press, Seaforth Publishing and White Owl

For a complete list of Pen & Sword titles please contact:

PEN & SWORD BOOKS LTD
47 Church Street, Barnsley, South Yorkshire, S70 2AS, UK.
E-mail: enquiries@pen-and-sword.co.uk
Website: www.pen-and-sword.co.uk

Or

PEN AND SWORD BOOKS,
1950 Lawrence Roadd, Havertown, PA 19083, USA
E-mail: Uspen-and-sword@casematepublishers.com
Website: www.penandswordbooks.com

Contents

PART I
152 (Hyderabad) Squadron

PART II
The Men of 152 (Hyderabad) Squadron

APPENDICES

FOREWORD

By Captain T. Baynham, DMM, MFC, SAAF
Son of the late Flying Officer G.T. Baynham

How perplexing are the ways of man! Despite our disputed mastery and supremacy over all earthly creatures, we have, since the beginning, consistently demonstrated an incongruous inability to co-exist in harmony with our own kind – man's deadliest enemy is man.

Indeed, this grim, tragic and bizarre legacy of our aggressive disposition lives on, and it is through conflict that mankind's destiny is ultimately forged.

From time immemorial, the course of history has been shaped by the outcome of great military campaigns waged on land, the high seas, and more recently in the skies. For generations, soldiers and sailors, on the eve of battle, have derived moral inspiration and fortitude from the recollection of past victories and the triumphant exploits of legendry heroes.

And so it is with today's airmen – eighty years ago, the Battle of Britain, dubbed the greatest air battle of all time, was fought and won by Fighter Command of the Royal Air Force, against the overwhelming power of the German Luftwaffe. Lest the passage of three quarters a century dim the memory, let us reflect on what was at stake in those dark hours of summer 1940. The world's largest air force, the Luftwaffe, having smashed the air forces of Poland, Norway, France, Holland and Belgium, turned its might and unbridled fury against the RAF as a prelude to the invasion and occupation of Britain by German forces. Charged with illusions of invulnerability in the wake of triumphs in Europe, the Luftwaffe predicted that the destruction of the already bruised and numerically inferior RAF Fighter Command could be accomplished within weeks with relatively little difficulty. However, as we know, this was not to be. Indeed, had the German Air Force succeeded in its objective, the face of history would probably have been very different today. The massive aerial onslaught launched against England between 10 July and 31 October 1940, was thwarted, in the main, by the extraordinary courage, and indomitable spirit of aircrews of Fighter Command. They remained undaunted by the grievously high battle casualties suffered and, against overwhelming odds, they preserved with an obstinacy and tenacity in the face of adversity that in the end led to victory – albeit by a narrow margin.

It was this miracle of effort that inspired Churchill to make his celebrated tribute to the unfaltering devotion of a mere 2,945 airmen: 'Never in the field of human conflict was so much, owed by so many, to so few.'

One of the supreme qualities of these young men – now known as 'The Few', was their refusal to take either their dangers or achievements seriously. A measure of their humility and frivolous spirit can be gauged from a comment heard in response to Churchill's famous eulogy, concerning who owed so much to whom – that he must have been referring to unpaid mess bills.

The Few would be the first to acknowledge that the Battle of Britain was not won in the air alone – it was won, too, in the factories, the repair shops, the maintenance units, the Flying Training Schools, the radar stations, operations rooms and a host of other places. And even in the air, it was the combined achievement of Bomber Command, Coastal Command and reconnaissance aircraft, as well as Fighter Command. But the public verdict has rightly acclaimed the pilots of Fighter Command as the foremost artisans of victory, for theirs was the responsibility and burden of front-line defence.

But who were these men? – these Few who upheld so magnificently the RAF motto – *Per Ardua ad Astra* – 'Through difficulties to the stars'? These men, whose courageous endeavours tipped the balance of fortune in Britain's favour, were ordinary young men, from all walks of life, who stood, united, shoulder to shoulder, in a common quest for liberty, in a time of dark and foreboding tyranny.

Although mainly British, they comprised many nationalities – Australians, New Zealanders, Poles, Czechs, the Free French, South Africans, Rhodesians, Canadians as well as others – thirteen nationalities in all. That the price of victory was high must not be forgotten. Some 507 airmen paid the supreme sacrifice and another 500 were wounded in combat during the battle.

And so we remember the Few – not with any sense of sadness, but with a sense of admiration, respect and pride, for the names of all of them are indelibly etched in the annals of history. Our memory of them will live on – and their gallantry will serve as an inspiration to future generations of fighter pilots, for they set an example that would be difficult to equal and almost impossible to surpass. Tomorrow's pilots must never forget that in war in the air, even more than on the land or the sea, the power of the weapon depends, in the end, upon the individual quality of the fighting man.

But may Almighty God, in his infinite and merciful wisdom, spare mankind from another world war, where young men might again be put to the ultimate test.

ACKNOWLEDGEMENTS

This is the first and probably the only book I will ever write. The only reason I have done this is because it has been my hobby for the last eight years, and in studying the men from 152 (Hyderabad) Squadron, they have become friends and not just a project.

They come from a bigger family and have many brothers all who fought on the same battlefield. But if I was to concentrate on them all I would never be able to finish this book in ten life times.

So, the following is just a small chapter out of a big book. Writing a book about a group of men who all showed an abundance of courage has been an amazing and immensely rewarding experience.

I am indebted to many people who have helped and offered me their time. I would first like to thank my wife, M, herself a RAF officer, for allowing me to spend many hours working on the computer to get this book completed. Andy Saunders, who has helped me from the start of my interest with more than enough material on the squadron to write his own book. He has been an inspiration and a great friend. The next friend I would like to thank is Richard Annis, for spending many a night on the telephone talking RAF shop to great annoyance from my better half.

Also, I would like to thank, in no particular order, Simon Muggleton, Rick Pemberry and Brian Puckett. All members of the Battle of Britain Historical Society, where I have been a proud member for a number of years and where I hope this book is especially enjoyed. The society's previous historian, the late Ted Sergison, must get a mention for all his time and interest in my research.

Alf Allsop, whose knowledge as a fitter with the squadron during the Battle of Britain, is still amazing and without his help the other side of squadron life could not be told.

Alan White, who has entrusted and given me many pictures of 152 Hyderabad Squadron.

Kristen Alexander for her expert knowledge of the Australians who flew during the Battle of Britain.

The RAF museum at Hendon, who has provided me with a large amount of information more than is in this book.

I cannot forget the heroes who I had the chance to meet to tell their stories of their own battle of survival and helped this book to come alive. It is a great honour to have met the following original pilots. My indebtedness goes in no set order: Wing Commander Charles Warren, Group Captain Peter Geoffrey St George O'Brian, Squadron Leader Norman Hancock, Flight Lieutenant Denis Robinson, and Squadron Leader Richard Inness.

Batting for the other team, my thanks must go to Chris Goss, Peter Cornwell, John Vasco, Brian Sadler and Philippa Hodgkiss, all having provided me with a greater understanding of the German aircraft and their crews who were shot down by 152 'Hyderabad' pilots.

The biggest mention must go to all the families of the men in question for their kindness in allowing me to learn of their personal accounts and their losses, which they have carried with them until this day.

To everybody above, my deepest thanks go to you as this book would never have been created without personal memoirs.

PREFACE

This book has stories and pictures that relate to the lives and flying experiences of forty men, some of whom were awarded medals in air combat over England in 1940. I have taken personal information and accounts from people who flew, or knew someone who flew, in the Battle of Britain and with the famous 152 Hyderabad Squadron.

I have attempted to make it a simple reference book with information relating to each pilot in question and a comprehensive look at the air warfare the squadron took part in on specific dates during the summer of 1940. In contrast, I have included information on German aircrews and their aircraft that were engaged by 152 Hyderabad Squadron.

I have tried to allow each pilot's account to be told separately, however there is some overlap. An example of this is where two pilots are attacking the same aircraft. When this occurs, I have clearly stated that this is the case.

The more I carried out my research the more my admiration grew, not just for 152 pilots but every airman who flew in the skies in the Battle of Britain, whether they be friend or foe.

ABBREVIATIONS

AA	Anti-Aircraft
A/C	Aircraft
AM	Air Ministry
ASR	Air Sea Rescue
BGS	B. & G. School Bombing and Gunnery School
BOAC	British Overseas Airways Corporation
CFI	Chief Flying Instructor
CFS	Central Flying School
CH	Chain Home (radar station)
CO	Commanding Officer
DFC	Distinguished Flying Cross
DFM	Distinguished Flying Medal
Do	Dornier
E/A, EA	Enemy Aircraft
EFTS	Elementary Flying Training School
E&RFTS	Elementary and Reserve Flying Training School
F.A.N.Y.	First Aid Nursing Yeomanry
F/Lt	Flight Lieutenant
F/O	Flying Officer
ft	Feet, Foot
FTS	Flying Training School
He	Heinkel
ITW	Initial Training Wing
Ju	Junkers
KW	Krzyż Walecznych (Polish: Cross of Valour)
Me	Messerschmitt
MTB	Motor Torpedo Boat
MO	Medical Officer
OC	Officer Commanding
ORB	Operations Record Book

OTU	Operational Training Unit
PAF	Polish Air Force
PO	Pilot Officer
RAAF	Royal Australian Air Force
RAF	Royal Air Force
RAFA	Royal Air Force Association
RAFO	Reserve of Air Force Officers
RAFVR	Royal Air Force Volunteer Reserve
R/T	Radio Telephone
SFTS	Service Flying Training School
Sgt.	Sergeant
S/Ldr	Squadron Leader
U/t	Under training
USAAF	United States Army Air Force

PART I
152 (Hyderabad) Squadron

The Nizam of Hyderabad, Mir Osman Ali Khan. (Author's Collection)

THE NIZAM OF HYDERABAD

Mir Osman Ali Khan, the seventh and the last Nizam of Hyderabad, ruled for thirty-seven years from 1911 to 1948. His dominion was larger than England and Scotland put together, with an area of 86,000 square miles.

The Nizam led a very simple life, yet he was one of the richest men in the world. He donated generously to every cause in India as well as abroad, irrespective of caste and religion. If it was the Muslim theological school at Deoband that received financial help, it was also the privilege of the Benaras Hindu University. His list of donations included Rabindranth Tagore's Shantiniketan and several other institutions, including hospitals, schools, for famine relief, etc. The Golden temple in Amritsar also enjoyed an annual donation.

The Nizam's rule saw the growth of Hyderabad economically and culturally, with electricity, railways, roads and airways also being developed. Huge reservoirs and irrigation projects such as the Tungabhadra and Nizamsagar were completed; the Osmania University, colleges and schools were founded throughout the state. Nearly all the public buildings, such as the Osmania General Hospital, High Court, Central State Library, Assembly Hall, Jubilee Hall and other buildings in the Public Garden, were built during Osman Ali Khan's reign.

Soon after India gained independence in 1947 all princely states were invited to join the Republic. Nizam VII was reluctant to do so; but in 1948 his state was merged into the Indian Union. Mir Osman Ali Khan, the last Nizam of Hyderabad, died on Friday, 24 February 1967.

Mark Andrew

RAF WARMWELL

In 1937, the Air Ministry announced it was to build an airfield near the small hamlet of Crossways 3 miles from the town of Dorchester, Dorset. This was to accommodate the RAF's need for a bombing and gunnery range and was to be the nearby Chesil beach, which is a long stretch of coastline running from Portland to Abbotsbury, considered to be an area of natural beauty.

Work was started, and RAF Woodsford, with No.6 Armament Training camp in situ, was officially opened on 1 May 1937. As the airfield was not yet complete, most of the airmen were billeted at the nearby Royal Armoured Corps, Bovington.

Throughout the following weeks aircraft began to appear, and in 1938 squadrons began arriving for their annual armament practice camps. The same year the airfield hosted its first Empire Air Day with instructors from surrounding fighter training schools joining pilots from the station to perform aerial displays for the public.

On 1 July 1938, RAF Woodsford was renamed RAF Warmwell, this title coming from the nearby village of Warmwell. It was done to avoid confusion with the Avro factory airfield at Woodford near Manchester.

The ranges were being frequently used with a number of 'Hard targets' being erected. The visits from various RAF, Auxiliary Air Force and even Fleet Air Arm squadrons increased throughout the late 1930s.

The year 1939 saw the second and last Empire Air Day at RAF Warmwell, because on 24 August, all reservists and Auxiliary Air Force personnel were called up for full-time service. On 1 November, No.10 Bombing and Gunnery school was formed at Warmwell and on 7 November the Central Gunnery School was established to instruct people in their specific roles.

With the outbreak of war the airfield was expanded in late 1939 to cover the nearby area of Knighton woods. RAF Warmwell came within the area of 10 Group with its HQ at Rudloe Manor, Box, Wiltshire.

Above: An aerial view of RAF Warmwell. Note that Knighton Woods can just be seen top left. (Author's Collection)

Below: After the war. the village of Crossways was created on part of the site of the former RAF Station Warmwell. This memorial in the village was commissioned to commemorate those who served at Warmwell and who died in the cause of freedom. (Courtesy of Mike Searle; www.geograph.org.uk)

However, it was not fully operational until August 1940, until which time Warmwell came under the control of 11 Group, commanded by Air Vice Marshal Keith Parks.

It was believed that the nearby naval base of Portland would be a 'high risk' target and that it would need to be defended. This could not be achieved from the new sector station at RAF Middle Wallop, which increased the need

Above: A distant shot of RAF Warmwell's hangars today. They are now used as farm storage. (Author's Collection)

Below: RAF Warmwell's Watch Office, now a private house. (Author's Collection)

for RAF Warmwell to be made a forward operating airfield, which was sanctioned by Fighter Command on 4 July 1940.

On 5 July, a flight from 609 (West Riding) Squadron arrived at RAF Warmwell, with 152 (Hyderabad) Squadron arriving on 11-12 July from RAF Acklington, Northumberland. This was to be the home of these two squadrons throughout the Battle of Britain.

The airfield received its fair share of enemy activity during 1940 when, on 25 August, the Luftwaffe bombed the airfield. Luckily there were no casualties, but the airfield received severe damage with its hangars and sick quarters receiving direct hits.

On 29 November, the rest of 609 (West Riding) Squadron transferred from RAF Middle Wallop to RAF Warmwell to take up full-time residence at the airfield.

The winter came with heavy snow well into 1941. The routine sorties continued against the Luftwaffe into the new year. No. 609 Squadron departed to its new home in 11 Group operating from RAF Biggin Hill, Kent, with the arrival of 234 Squadron from RAF St Eval, Cornwall.

Again, RAF Warmwell was attacked by the Luftwaffe on 26 March with no casualties occurring. This was repeated on 1 April, when the enemy dropped a mass of bombs onto the airfield. Sadly, on this occasion there were a number of fatalities and many wounded. There was much destruction to the structure of buildings on the airfield with damage to the hangars and a number of aircraft.

Hyderabad Squadron was given warning that it would be moving to RAF Portreath, Cornwall. This happened on 9 April 1941, and two months later the Central Gunnery School departed to its new home at RAF Castle Kennedy, Scotland. In November 1942, 402 (City of Winnipeg) Squadron RCAF arrived at the airfield to carry out offensive sweeps over the English Channel against enemy shipping. It remained at RAF Warmwell until its departure in March 1942 to RAF Colerne, Wiltshire.

The same month saw the formation of 175 Squadron, which was made up of mostly Commonwealth pilots. Their aircraft were 'Hurribombers', a Hurricane Mk IIB fighter able to carry a bomb-load. They carried out a number of operational sorties including attacks at Dieppe, France, in 1942 in support of the disastrous Canadian amphibious operation. They remained at RAF Warmwell until their move to RAF Harrowbeer, Devon, in October that year.

Many more squadrons arrived at Warmwell throughout 1942, with 263 Squadron flying the impressive Westland Whirlwind, arriving on

RAF Warmwell's station cinema, now a village hall. (Author's Collection)

7 September to carry out *Rhubarb* and anti-shipping sorties over the English Channel and French coast for the remaining period of the year.

The year 1942 also saw the arrival of 266 Squadron on 8 September, flying Typhoons. It carried out operational sorties, intercepting enemy aircraft approaching the English coast. It undertook a number of offensive sweeps over the French coast, attacking rail locomotives and enemy troop convoys.

The beginning of 1943 saw the departure of 266 Squadron with another Typhoon squadron arriving in the form of 257 Squadron from RAF Exeter, Devon, on 8 January to carry out similar duties to their predecessors.

Due to bad weather conditions, the airfield was placed non-operational on occasion throughout 1943.

It was in 1944 when the 474th Fighter Group USAAF arrived at RAF Warmwell, assuming command of the airfield in February that year. It was equipped with P-38 Lightings and, with this, for the third time the airfield changed its name, this time to 454 USAAF Moreton. Training continued with its new pilots and ground crews during the early months of 1944, conducting escort missions to heavy bomber formations over countries such France, and Denmark.

A historic day for the airfield was on 6 June 1944, with the 474th carrying out numerous operations over the French coast destroying specific targets in support of Operation *Overlord*. On 5 August, command was given back to the RAF with the departure of the 474th Fighter Group to a new home at Neuilly, France.

The armament practice camps continued with the formation of 17 and 14 APC, with many squadrons attending right up until 1945, when the APC units were disbanded. After the war, RAF Warmwell became a demobilisation centre for RAF families who had been trapped in foreign countries.

In the 1960s-70s, the former airfield was purchased by EEC quarries and used for gravel extraction with other areas of the airfield used for housing development. It now portrays a different life to the 1940s, and is covered in large craters for the use of the quarries with only a few buildings standing to show that it was once a key location in the Battle of Britain.

152 (HYDERABAD) SQUADRON DURING THE BATTLE OF BRITAIN

During the First World War the Nizam of Hyderabad donated a Squadron of D.H.9As to the Air Ministry. It replied to the prince thanking him for his 'generous gift' stating that his name would be forever linked with a squadron of the RAF. On the outbreak of the Second World War the Nizam enquired what 'his' squadron would be doing?

The Air Ministry embarrassingly explained that the name 'Hyderabad' had long been forgotten and his original donation would cover the cost of only two modern fighters. So, the Nizam promptly stumped up the funding for the cost of a modern fighter squadron, and a full complement of aircraft. This being the total sum of £100,000. His name was given as an official title to No.152 Squadron gaining the motto of 'Faithful Ally' officially on 26 November 1939. 152 'Hyderabad' Squadron was the first RAF squadron to receive presentation aircraft. The Nizam also sent a donation of £60 to the squadron to allow the pilots to hold a party. The pilots believed he could have been a little more generous!

Originally, 152 Squadron had been formed on 18 October 1918 as a night fighter squadron during the First World War, but it was disbanded in June 1919.

On the outbreak of the Second World War the squadron was reformed as a fighter squadron on 1 October 1939. Based at RAF Acklington, Northumberland, under the command of Squadron Leader F.W.C. Shute, it was initially equipped with Gloster Gladiators, though much of the initial flying also involved Avro Tutors and Hawker Harts. Within weeks, the squadron began re-equipping with Mk.I Spitfires, becoming operational on 6 January 1940.

The squadron's primary role was to carry out coastal patrols and convoy escort sorties, protecting such vessels as the great battleship

Right: The 152 (Hyderabad) Squadron crest. (Courtesy RAF Museum)

King George V. On one occasion, a flight from the squadron escorted Lord Louis Mountbatten's ship HMS *Kelly* into Liverpool docks. For its efforts, he sent a personal thank you message to the squadron.

There were twelve pilots, half of whom were sergeant pilots and the other half were commissioned from the RAFVR as pilot officers. There was a small number of pilots who had seen service in the RAF before the outbreak of hostilities.

The squadron's first combat came over the North Sea on 29 January 1940. The squadron's first confirmed 'kill' came five days later, on 3 February. Under the headline 'Indian Gift That Has an Effect in North Sea', the event was reported in the national press:

> The fighter squadron formed with the £100,000 gift from the Nizam of Hyderabad to the Royal Air Force has shot down its first enemy aircraft. It is the first of the newly formed fighter squadrons to do so.

Below: HMS *Kelly* underway. (Author's Collection)

Above: Squadron stores arriving at RAF Warmwell. (Author's Collection)

Below: The pilots of 152 Squadron pictured soon after their arrival at RAF Warmwell. Left to right they are: Pilot Officer Charles Warren, Sergeant Ralph Wolton, Pilot Officer Boy Marrs, Sergeant Eric Shepperd, Pilot Officer Richard Inness, Flight Lieutenant Latham Withall, Pilot Officer Tim Wildblood, Flying Officer Christopher Deanesly, Pilot Officer John Jones, Flight Lieutenant Frederick Thomas (on back), Pilot Officer Dudley Williams, Pilot Officer Ian Bayles, Sergeant Harold Ackroyd, and P/O Pooch. (Author's Collection)

The victim was one of the three Heinkels [He 111s] brought down during raids on shipping on February 3. The machine crashed into the sea in Creswell Bay, Northumberland. Three of the crew took to their rubber boat, but the high seas gave them no chance. Their bodies were washed ashore.

As a souvenir of the combat, the rubber boat is now housed in the squadron's rest room. Pieces of wreckage from the Heinkel have strewn the shore, and the pilots of the victorious squadron have been given some of the bullet-riddled metal as souvenirs. One large piece is to be beaten into a shield and engraved with the squadron's crest.

Nearly all the Dominions, as well as Great Britain, are represented along the pilots.

The commanding officer is a native of Woolwich. He led the attack on the Heinkel and gave it the coup de grace.

In July 1940 with German attacks increasing against Allied shipping in the English Channel and coastal ports such as Portsmouth and the Royal Navy base at Portland, Air Vice Marshal Sir Christopher Quintin Brand, officer commanding 10 Group with his HQ at Rudloe Manor. requested a fighter squadron that would have the primary role of defending these vital ports and shipping lanes off the south coast.

On 11 July, the squadron transport left Acklington for its new home at RAF Warmwell. The remaining squadron aircraft departed on the morning of 12 July, under the new commanding officer, Squadron Leader Peter Devitt.

RAF Warmwell was situated 3 miles from the coast and in close to the coastal town of Weymouth. The grass airfield was a small satellite station for 10 Group's sector airfield, RAF Middle Wallop. The first Spitfire touched its wheels down at Warmwell with a welcome of low cloud and typical Dorset rain. The airfield was crowded with Wellingtons and Harrow aircraft that departed the next day.

Pilot Officer Dennis Fox-Male remembers his time at Warmwell:

The buildings were luxurious compared to 1939-45 concrete stations. The Officers Mess and living quarters were to the east of the road through the station and with hangars and administrative blocks to the west. Beyond there on the Dorchester side was the grass airfield, long and narrow. Take-off and landing were almost always along this east-west axis to the east over the hangars and

Above: Squadron flying in formation. (Author's Collection)

Below: The moment one of the squadron's Spitfires, UM-A, lands back at Warmwell. The pilot on this occasion was Squadron Leader Peter Devitt. (Author's Collection)

buildings, or to the west over a thick wood of firs and other trees about 20-30 feet high. If the wind was strong it was possible to land about 20 degrees off this axis but the airfield was not rectangular and had a 'waist' which prevented landing at right angles to the main axis.

Warmwell station personnel were all concerned with air gunnery in July 1940. The gunnery school was not concerned with the war. It concentrated on drogue-towing by Blenheims with air gunners firing from Wellingtons. This took place several miles off the coast until a Blenheim was shot down in error by fighters from a neighbouring sector and it was reluctantly agreed that the gunnery lines would be inland. Yet until the end of 1940 by which time two fighter squadrons were stationed there, Warmwell considered itself a gunnery school under the late Group Captain George Howard, DFC. He is known for his classic remark he made to 609 squadron, 'When I was in a fighter squadron we were never late for our meals'.

The men did not have long to get settled in at their new home. On 13 July, they scrambled to intercept a raid over Portland with Flight Lieutenant Withall claiming to have damaged a Ju88 south of Warmwell.

The squadron consisted of twelve operational aircraft and a few spare. The squadron was split into two flights 'A' and 'B'. This would then be split down further into sections. 'A' Flight consisted of Red, Yellow and White sections while 'B' Flight comprised Blue, Green and Black sections. 'A' Flight would always lead a squadron scramble with 'A' Flight commander deciding what formation he wanted the rest of the aircraft to be in. The normal take-off position would always be in Vic formation whether it was a squadron or flight taking off.

Red 1

Red 2   White 1

Yellow 1   White 2

Yellow 2   **'A' Flight**

Blue 1

Blue 2   Black 1

Green 1   Black 2

Green 2   **'B' Flight**

Above: UM-L taxiing to a halt after landing at Warmwell. (Author's Collection)

Below: The squadron dispersal at Warmwell. (Author's Collection)

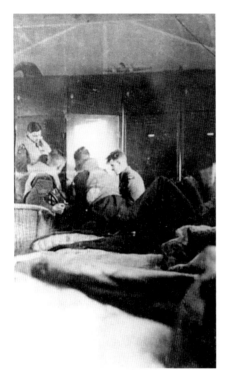

Red 1 would form the spearhead of the Vic formation with Red 2 to his immediate left, followed by Yellow 1 and Yellow 2. On his right would be White 1 and White 2. Once in the air, Red 2 would fall in behind Red 1, Yellow 2 behind Yellow 1, and White 1 with White 2 behind him. 'B' Flight would do the same when in the air.

Flights would form themselves into two files of three machines in a Vic formation. Or in case of the squadron formation, two ranks of six forming a Vic formation. When in the air, the sector controllers would talk the squadron onto enemy formations using their radio call-sign 'Mandrake' and the squadron radio call-sign of 'Maida'.

Above: Inside the 'B' Flight dispersal hut at Warmwell. (Author's Collection)

Below: A pencil drawing of Spitfires from 152 Squadron.

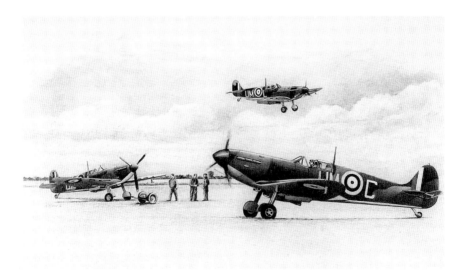

Above: A typical scene at Warmwell in the summer of 1940. In this picture, from left to right, are Boy Marrs, John Jones, Tim Wildblood and Doug Shepley. P/O Pooch can be seen in the foreground. (Author's Collection)

Below: A small group of pilots at Warmwell. On the left is Dudley Williams, while Boy Marrs is on the right. The individual in the centre has not been identified. (Author's Collection)

Life at an operational fighter station was like any other during those hectic months of the Battle of Britain in 1940. With the intense heat, pilots would sit outside dispersal in deckchairs and armchairs playing chess or reading a book, just waiting for the telephone to ring and the cry of 'scramble!' Pilot Officer Roger Hall remembers the dispersal hut:

> Dispersal was a wooden hut with a telephone and an orderly constantly attending it. This was the telephone that gave us instructions to scramble. There were twelve beds, ordinary iron beds with mattresses and blankets arranged on the two sides of the hut. The pilots rested on them when they were at readiness or even slept on them for the remainder of the night after a pub crawl. To come straight down to dispersal on arrival back from the pub crawl and get into bed was to ensure that one was there for readiness at dawn.

On the squadron dispersal hut hung a sign would hang from the main door saying 'Joe Guppy's Camp'. This sign belonged to a local farmer who encouraged pre-war campers to use his land near Weymouth. This sign had obviously been 'liberated' on one of the many squadron nights out.

Pilot Officer Dennis Fox-Male recalls:

> Dispersal for 152 was a long wooden hut in the north-western corner of the airfield near the trees. Access was over a track through a field to the north of the airfield. For a short time 'A' Flight moved to a site on the south of the field but this was not a success and morale in the squadron was even better when both flights shared the same hut.

A game would be played by the pilots while waiting at dispersal, all taking part would have to wear a tin helmet. Someone would throw a brick up into the air and they would all then huddle together and whoever the brick lands on is the person who gets to throw it into the air on the next occasion.

Each squadron would have an adjutant. His job would be to deal with clerical administration and looking after the squadron's interests on the ground. Flying Officer Laverack was the squadron's adjutant from its reformation in 1939. He was known by all as the 'adj' and is remembered fondly by Pilot Officer Roger Hall:

19

13: The squadron's adjutant, Flying Officer Laverack, dressed in flying clothing. (Author's Collection)

Above: A profile of one of 152 Squadron's Spitfires, coded UM B. (Author's Collection)

He was a middle-aged man who had seen service as a soldier in the previous war. He was one of the many who having been a regular soldier was axed when he was too young to retire, and found sanctuary and comradeship in the administrative branch of the RAF.

When I entered his office, he spoke to me as father to son and made certain I had everything I needed. In the ante-room I met the Adj again and he asked me what I was going to have. We had a pint each and I asked him to tell me about the Squadron and what they had done since they had been down there.

Below: A Messerschmitt Bf 109 flying low over RAF Warmwell. (Author's Collection)

Above: The pilots of 152 Squadron. In the back row, left to right, are: Mr Carr, Sergeant Berry, Sergeant Cassell, Flight Sergeant Bowen, Warrant Officer Hill, Flight Sergeant Barnes, Flight Sergeant Hutton, Sergeant Walker and Sergeant Frost. In the middle row, again left to right, are: Sergeant Akroyd, Sergeant Sheppard, Pilot Officer Hogg, Pilot Officer McBain, Pilot Officer Bayles, Pilot Officer Watson, Pilot Officer Beaumont, Pilot Officer Warren, Pilot Officer Marrs, Pilot Officer Holmes, Sergeant Barker and Sergeant Reddington. In the front row, left to right, are: Sergeant Robinson, Pilot Officer Wildblood, Flying Officer Laverack (Adjutant), Flying Officer O'Brien, Flight Lieutenant Boitel-Gill, Squadron Leader Devitt, Flight Lieutenant Thomas, Flying Officer Hogg, Flying Officer Deverell, Pilot Officer Cox, and Sergeant Holland. P/O Pooch, the squadron mascot, is in the foreground. (Author's Collection)

Pilot Officer Richard Inness also remembers Flying Officer Laverack well: 'You could always find him; he was in the bar or in his room recovering from a long night in the mess!'

As the months went on, the faces of the squadron began to change and they were all arriving with very little experience flying Spitfires and it was left to the pilots who had some combat flying time to train these young men. But no matter how little time one of the pilots had

Above: A group photograph of 'A' Flight personnel. (Author's Collection)

done in the squadron they all got along with each other. When in the air, they had to rely on each other as at any time an enemy fighter could dive down out of nowhere and it was up to someone to shout on the R/T, 'Look out behind, snappers, break'.

On an evening, they would go to the local pubs and try and forget about their day's life-threatening experiences. On their return at normally around 02.00 hours they were often in a semi-conscious state. On one occasion Flying Officer Graham Cox was returning to the airfield in his large Humber car with a number of other pilots after a night out in nearby Bournemouth. Taking the road back to the airfield, he reached the Moreton railway station level crossing. With the gates slowly going down he decided he would take these gates on and accelerate.

The gates must have been very sturdy and did not suffer but his car did somewhat.

Another occasion clearly remembered by Leading Aircraftsman Burns, who during the Battle of Britain was an armourer with the squadron, was when he was watching a group of pilots leaving the mess one evening.

Above: The personnel of 152 Squadron's 'B' Flight. (Author's Collection)

There had been built static water tanks for use by the station fire brigade and these were covered with a camouflaged net. After a party in the mess fun and games began to be played. A group of pilots would hold the net tightly and one would attempt to walk across. However, on reaching the middle all who were holding the net would release it and of course a good ducking was had by the walker of course which was no surprise.

Pilot Officer Dennis Fox-Male remembers:

The party went on until 1am when we drove back direct to dispersal because we were at readiness section at dawn. We staggered into the hut and flopped down on our beds, flat out in a few minutes. It was not long after dawn in the morning when the telephone rang and we were scrambled and ordered to the Isle of Wight.

There was a noticeable difference between 152 and 609 squadrons in both dress and discipline as some of the photographs of that time show. Some Hyderabad men can be seen wearing Sidcot suits while others are wearing four-pocket tunics. This was not tolerated by the station commander who often approached Squadron Leader Peter Devitt asking if he could 'sort his chaps out'. But nothing did change. On one

Above : Squadron ground crew. (Author's Collection)

occasion, for example, a Royal Artillery officer who was in charge of the anti–aircraft positions approached two of 152 Squadron's pilots, one of whom was Pilot Officer 'Boy' Marrs. The artillery officer attempted to reprimand Marrs over his standard of dress, only to receive an unpleasant reply from Boy who just continued to walk on past.

This account gives some indication of squadron life during the Battle of Britain. The subsequent chapters will detail the actions of each of the squadron's forty pilots at one of the most critical moments in the history of the British Isles.

152 (HYDERABAD) SQUADRON OPERATION RECORDS BOOK FOR THE BATTLE OF BRITAIN

Please note that the following transcript is reproduced in the form that it was originally written. There are a number of spelling mistakes and typographical errors in the entries, leading to inconsistencies in the text, which have been retained for historical accuracy.

JULY

WARMWELL
1		No operational flying.
2		No operational flying.
3	12.15	Given section to patrol – Farne Is. Angels 5.
	13.10	Given section landed.
4		No operational flying.
5		No operational flying.
6		No operational flying.
7	08.32	Green Section to Patrol Holy Is. Angels 8.
8		No operational flying.
9		No operational flying.
10		No operational flying.
11		Yellow and Red Sections patrolled convoy off Farne Is. 13 Group rung up to tell us we had to go to Warmwell to protect Portland which at that time had been having some fairly heavy blows.
12		Squadron led by S/Ldr Devitt flew from Acklington to Warmwell, starting in perfect weather and finishing in very

low rain cloud at Warmwell. Remainder of personnel came by special train. The aerodrome was covered in Harrow and Wellington aircraft of No. 10 B. & G. School. These went the next day which left the aerodrome a bit clearer. C.G.S. remained which kept the drome still fairly blocked.

13 There were several air raids during this day and combats took place. F/Lt. Withall attacked an E/A but without result.

14 Several air raids during day but no combats took place.

15 Several air raids during day but no combats took place.

16 Several Air Raids during day but no combats took place.

17 F/Lt. Withall fired all his ammunition into a JU.88 but it did not apparently have any effect.

18 During an air raid P/O Bayles had a combat with an ME.109 who fired at him without success. He also had a combat with 3 ME.109's when on patrol over convoy but by taking evasive action he was able to shake them off on returning to base it was found there were several bullet holes in his machine. P/O. Warren also was engaged by 2 E.A and also sustained bullet holes in his machine. P/O Hogg also fired all his ammunition at a DO.215 but without apparent result.

19 Several air raids during day but no combats took place.

20 In the course of several air raids P/O Inness had a combat with 2 ME.109's. He fired at one but without any definite results.

21 Several air raids but no combats.

22 Several air raids but no combats.

23 Several air raids but no combats.

24 Several air raids but no combats.

25 11.15 The Squadron took off at 1050 hours and patrolled Portland. At 1115 hours a large number of enemy aircraft, estimated to be 18 JU.87, 12 ME.109 and 1 DO.17 was spotted about 20 miles south of Portland flying north west at 10,000 feet to 11,000 feet. The aircraft of the squadron operated in pairs. When getting within range, "B" Flight attacked the formation of ME.109's which was above and acting as a rear-guard to the JU.87's and the DO.17. "A" Flight intended to attack the bombers but were immediately attacked by the ME.109's. A dog-fight followed. F/O. Deansley, P/O. Hogg and Sgt. Walton attacked the DO.17 (No. 1. attack). Cannon

fire was experienced from the rear gun. F/O. Deansley fired all his rounds but was brought down in the sea. He was picked up by a trawler and landed at Lyme Regis. Sgt. Walton and P/O Holmes also fired at this E/A which came down near Fleet. Sgt. Walton and P/O Hogg also attacked a JU.87 at which they both fired the rest of their ammunition. The E/A dived steeply and No. 110 Searchlight Battery at Portland reported that a JU.87 crashed nearby into the sea at the time of the combat. P/O Inness attacked a ME.109 from above and the quarter. He climbed after the E/A for 1000 feet, firing again at 100 yards. The E/A dived vertically down, but Inness could not follow as he had to take evasive action from 2 ME.109's which dived on his tail. S/Ldr. Devitt attacked a ME.109, but he himself was attacked from the rear and the tail of his a/c was hit by cannon shot. He turned sharply and was unable to see what happened to the ME.109.

26	Several patrols but no combats.
27	Several patrols but no combats. F/Lt. Boitel-Gill rejoined his Squadron.
28	Several patrols but no combats.
29	Several patrols but no combats.
30	Several patrols but no combats.
31	Several patrols but no combats.

AUGUST

1	Several patrols but no combats.
2	Several patrols but no combats.
3	Several patrols but no combats.
4	Several patrols but no combats.
5	Several patrols but no combats.
6	Several patrols but no combats.
7	Several patrols but no combats.
8	During 1 raid P/O. Wildblood joined 3 Hurricanes chasing a ME.109 to the French coast. They passed the ME.109 and fired a short burst at 400 yards, but apparently without result. Sgt. Robinson was attacked from behind by a ME.109 and he felt bullets striking his machine. He dived down 6000 feet and when pulling out of dive found his machine U/S and then force-landed near Langton MacTravers. P/O.

Shipley encountered 10 ME.109's. He opened fire on one of them and when he broke away black smoke was pouring from it and bits were coming off his tail which had been seriously damaged. F/O. Hogg attacked 2 ME.109's one after the other and black smoke was seen coming from the tail of one of them. He then made further attacks on ME.109's but these were ineffective as he himself was attacked. P/O. Beaumont when attacking a ME.109 was attacked by another, his cockpit filled with smoke and he went down out of control and force-landed. Neither Sgt. Robinson nor P/O. Beaumont were injured.

9   Various patrols were made but no combats.

10   Various patrols were made but no combats. Blue and Black Sections went to Middle Wallop for night flying.

MIDDLE WALLOP

11   Four Spitfires took off from Middle Wallop to proceed to Warmwell, being vectored to a point between Swanage and Portland. 18 109's were sighted in a dog fight with either Spitfires or Hurricanes. They broke up and started back to France. S/Ldr. Devitt and P/O. Williams chased them but were unable to get into effective range. S/Ldr. Devitt fired a few rounds at about 500 yards but without apparent result. P/O. Wildblood attacked a ME.109 and closed to fifty yards, and this E/A was seen to dive vertically into the sea, he then turned to attack another ME.109 together with P/O. Shipley he fired remainder of ammunition and then broke away leaving P/O. Shipley to continue attack. Black smoke was seen coming from this machine which dived fast and steadily downwards. F/Lt. Boitel-Gill saw P/O. Jones bail out and parachute open, but unfortunately no more was heard of P/O. Jones who was therefore reported missing.

12   In a patrol over St. Catherine's Point, P/O. Hogg and P/O. Beaumont intercepted 12 JU.88. P/O. Beaumont attacked one of them and put his starboard engine out of action. P/O. Hogg saw a machine go into the sea. P/O. Hogg and P/O. Beaumont attacked another machine and observed a large piece of metal fall off this E/A. P/O. Hogg was convinced that this machine would be compelled to force-land in the

Isle of Wight. Sgt. Shepperd encountered 12 JU.88's. He attacked one of them and P/O. Bayles saw the port engine in flames. He then attacked another and expended all his ammunition. He followed this machine down and saw it land in a field and burst into flames. P/O. Wildblood attacked a ME.109 and got in one burst of fire but with unknown result. He then attacked a ME.111 which went down in an inverted spiral dive but did not see it actually crash. F/Lt. Boitel-Gill attacked an E/A which burst into flames and crashed. He then fired at another which flew through his burst but did not catch fire. He then attacked another machine but did not see result of attack. P/O. Hogg attacked a JU.88. He fired all his rounds and this machine was seen to crash into the sea. Unfortunately F/Lt. Withall and P/O. Shipley failed to return.

WARMWELL

13   In a patrol over Portland P/O. Inness attacked a ME.110 and his starboard engine belched black smoke and pieces flew off and was last seen losing height into cloud. He then attacked another ME110 and was attacked by a ME.110 one of whose bullets pierced his armour plating and wounded him in the arm (slight). F/Lt. Boitel-Gill led an attack on a formation of 30 ME.110's. He did not see any actual machine go down but was of the opinion that as his formation was so light that some damage must have been done. P/O. Beaumont attacked a ME.110 but had to make evasive action as another ME.110 was on his tail. He then attacked another which dived vertically into cloud. P/O. Warren attacked 3 ME.110's but without result. P/O. Cox attacked a ME.110 which turned on its back and dived vertically into cloud. P/O. Bayles also attacked a ME.110 and smoke was seen coming from its port engine. P/O. Williams attacked a ME.110 and was also attacked. He turned on his back and seeing what he thought was a ME.110 on his tail he continued diving into cloud.

Whilst on patrol over Portland F/Lt. Boitel-Gill led an attack on a large formation of JU.87's. He fired on one which broke up in the air. He then attacked two ME.110's both of which burst into flames. His own machine was extremely badly damaged. His bringing it back to base was undoubtedly a magnificent effort. P/O. Hogg carried out three attacks on this same formation but without apparent result. Sgt. Shepherd attacked this formation but without visible result. He then attacked a single machine from another formation, which was damaged and had broken away. He could not say if it was definitely destroyed. Sgt. Barker also attacked this formation and he reports that fire ceased from the rear gunner of the machine he attacked. He then attacked a ME.110 and it went into a steep spiral dive with smoke coming from both engines. He did not see it hit the sea. P/O. Marrs attacked a JU.87 and also had a dog fight with a ME.110 without result. Sgt. Ackroyd attacked a JU.87 and saw his perspex splinter and the machine went down from formation. He followed it down but was then attacked and his machine was so much damaged and his rudder jammed, he returned to base. Sgt. Robinson attacked a ME.109 which he followed down and saw burst into flames and crash in a wood near Abbotsbury.

14	Several patrols but no combats.
15	Several patrols but no combats.
16	During a patrol over Ventnor P/O. Beaumont spotted 12 ME.109's. He informed F/Lt. Thomas. He then broke away and saw 3 ME.109's. He climbed up behind and then opened fire and smoke was seen pouring from the machine which slowly turned on its back and dived vertically. The other two machines immediately dived towards France. He followed one and opened fire. This machine staggered and bits came off, and there is no doubt it crashed into the sea.
18	Eleven Aircraft went to intercept a raid approaching Portsmouth. South of the Isle of Wight the Squadron dived from 4,000 feet to attack a force of 30 JU.87's flying south near sea level. Red 1, F/Lt. Boitel-Gill sent one E/A into the sea attacked three others and was himself attacked probably by an HE.113. Red 2, P/O. Holmes also destroyed a JU.87. Yellow 2, Sgt. Shepperd, closing to 50 yards sent another JU.87 into the sea and then finished his ammunition on another JU.87 but was unable to see any resulting damage. By this time ME.109's had appeared and White 1, P/O. Cox,

Above : One of 152 Squadron's Spitfires, in this case UM-N, pictured at dispersal. (Author's Collection)

having attacked a JU.87 without result broke away upwards to attack a ME.109 which was on the tail of a Spitfire. Blue 1, P/O. Beaumont, attacked the same ME.109 which dived into the sea. White 2, Sgt. Barker, dived behind White 1 at the beginning of the engagement, and attacked a JU.87 from the upper port quarter, closing from 200 to 40 yards. The E/A which was about 50 feet above the sea, dived in. Blue 1, P/O. Beaumont and Blue 2, P/O. Williams each destroyed a JU.87. Black 1, P/O. Wildblood sent one JU.87 into the sea and then helped some Hurricanes and Spitfires to destroy another. Black 2, P/O. Marrs by a deflection burst set fire to the port wing of a JU.87 which dived into the sea.

The Squadron losses were 2 A/C temporarily unserviceable with no loss of personnel. The enemy lost 9 JU.87's and 1 ME.109.

22 16.50 Red Section, P/O. Cox, P/O. Hogg and P/O. Holmes encountered a JU.88 off the Needles. The section attacked

Above: UM-M photographed at dispersal waiting for a 'scramble'. Note the tent in the background. (Author's Collection)

from above and astern and Red 1 opened fire at 250 yards. No. 1 attack was employed. The JU.88 dived down to about 10 feet above the sea and crashed half a minute later. Red 2 had his A/C temporarily unserviceable owing to shots from the enemy rear gun.

17.17 Blue section went up from Warmwell at 1717 hours. Blue 2, P/O. Watson became separated from the others. He climbed to 25,000 feet and attacked one of two JU.88 10 miles south of Portland. Pieces flew off the port engine and Blue 2 followed it down to 5,000 feet. Blue 1 P/O. Marrs and Blue 3 P/O. Warren attacked a DO.17 which was making for the coast near Portland. Both attacked it and although they did not see it crash, the Observer Corps reported a DO.17 in the sea and there is no doubt that it was the E/A attacked by Blue 1 and 3.

25 12 A/C took off at 1657. Warmwell was bombed and afterwards between 1720 and 1725 about 20 JU.88's, 30 ME.110's and 40 ME.109's were encountered west of

Portland. The engagement became a collection of dog fights in which P/O. Marrs (Black 2) destroyed a ME.110, P/O. Beaumont (Green 2) destroyed a ME.109, Sgt. Barker (White 2) destroyed a ME.109 and F/Lt. Thomas (Blue 1) probably destroyed a JU.88. F/O. Deansley and P/O. O'Brian went up from Warmwell when it was bombed, but they did not engage. P/O. Hogg and P/O. Wildblood were lost in this engagement.

27 Green Section, P/O. Beaumont and F/O. O'Brian destroyed a HE.111 west of Portland. They were at 12,000 feet and dived 2,000 feet to attack the E/A from astern. A chase followed in and out of cloud and eventually the E/A dived into the sea. Green 1, P/O. Beaumont, had to bale out and landed at Portland.

SEPTEMBER

4 3 A/C of Yellow section, flying at 19,000 feet over Bognor Regis, saw a DO.17 1,000 feet below. They followed the E/A and attacked it at 5,000 feet. 25 miles S.S.E. of Bognor Regis Sgt. Barker had to bale out and was lost. No claim was made in respect of E/A.

7 10.30 2 A/C Green section (P/O. Beaumont and Sgt. Christie) when at 20,000 feet over Lyme Regis saw a DO.215 10 miles out to sea going south. The section gave chase. The Dornier dived to sea level and the section attacked 10 miles south of Portland. Green 1 carried out quarter attacks and astern attacks and at the third burst the enemy's starboard engine emitted white smoke which was still seen as the E/A flew out of sight in the direction of the Channel Islands. Green 2 was only able to give one short burst from astern as the E/A was so near the sea that he had to break away.

15 6 aircraft "B" flight, No. 152 Squadron on patrol sighted 30 Heinkel 111 7 miles S.W. of Portland at 15,000 feet proceeding N.W. Enemy aircraft were flying in vics of 3 stepped up in an irregular line astern, and had no fighter escort. Enemy aircraft turned N.E. The flight passed the enemy aircraft on an opposite course and N.W. of it. The enemy aircraft formation turned S.E. after attacking Portland. Our attack commenced 5 miles S.E. of Portland. Green section 3 aircraft

carried out attack on a straggler from enemy formation. Green 1 (F/O. O'Brian) made an astern attack concentrating fire on starboard engine, broke away left and downwards. Green 3 (Sgt. Holland) then attacked with 5 secs. burst from astern and above, and black smoke poured from starboard engine and it began to lose height. Green 2 (P/O. Watson) then attacked same enemy aircraft with 5 secs. burst, saw smoke coming from both engines and undercarriage falling. Green 1 again attacked and saw considerable smoke from starboard engine. Green 2 attacked another straggler at 8,000 feet and after 8 secs. burst, enemy aircraft blew to pieces in the air and fell into the sea about 15 miles S.W. of Swanage. Blue section attacked aircraft on extreme left of the rearmost enemy section. Blue 1 (P/O. Marrs) attacked from astern and broke away downwards. Blue 2 (Sgt. Christie) attacked this enemy aircraft from astern slightly to the starboard. Blue 1 then came up underneath and made No. 2 attack on right hand aircraft of enemy formation, which was straggling and after making another astern attack, broke off the combat as section was setting too far out to sea. The flight landed at Warmwell at 1555 hours.

17   13.50   3 Aircraft of Blue section, No. 152 Squadron, on patrol at 15,000 feet over Portland Bill were vectored to Junkers 88 at 17,000 feet which was flying north over Shepton Mallet. The section first sighted enemy aircraft when a mile away and carried out No. 1 attack. Enemy aircraft dived steeply for cloud at 6,000 feet. Blue 1 (P/O. Marrs), 2 (Sgt. Holland) 3 (F/O. O'Brian) then attacked individually as opportunity arose, and white smoke was seen coming from starboard engine of enemy aircraft. The engine of Blue 1 aircraft seized when it was hit by machine gun from enemy aircraft, and Blue 1 landed at Colerne Aerodrome, where he found a bullet hole through his oil cooler. Meanwhile Blue 2 and 3 continued to attack enemy aircraft concentrating on starboard engine until Blue 3 saw engine stopped, when smoke almost ceased. Blue 3 then attacked with full deflection concentrating fire from below on the right wing of enemy aircraft and his final attack was made in cloud from port rear quarter of enemy aircraft.

During the last two attacks no return fire was seen. Blue 2 and 3 then lost enemy aircraft in thick cloud going on southerly course, and searched above and below cloud but without success. Engine of Blue 2 became hot so he landed at Yatesbury Aerodrome and found that his aircraft had been hit by machine gun fire in 3 places. Enemy aircraft crashed at Chitterne. Blue 3 landed Warmwell 1425 hours, Blue 1 landed Colerne, Blue 2 landed at Yatesbury.

19   Green section, 2 aircraft, No. 152 Squadron up from Warmwell were vectored to Junkers 88 at 10,000 feet over the Channel. R/T of Green 1 (P/O. Williams) was unserviceable and when he became separated from Green 2 he returned to Warmwell. Green 2 (Sgt. Holland) saw Junkers 88 ahead on the right, two miles away. The interception was due almost entirely to the excellent instructions given by the Controller. Green 2 gave chase and made alternate quarter attacks from left and right from 300 to 200 yards aiming first at gunners position and then at each engine. Enemy aircraft took slight evasive action but mainly concentrated on heading for cloud in a southerly direction. Return fire ceased after the first attack. White and black puffs of smoke began to appear after the second attack. Green 2 continued to attack and eventually the enemy aircraft which was now at about 8,000 feet dived vertically towards the sea with both engines on fire. As his ammunition was now finished and his engine was missing slightly Green 2 flew north landing at Portsmouth Aerodrome. He there checked his engine, found it to be in order, and returned to Warmwell.

25   12 Spitfires, No. 152 Squadron went up from Warmwell between 1000 and 1020 hours to intercept large formation of enemy bombers which were crossing the coast west of Portland. The enemy force consisted of a mixed formation of 60 Junkers 88 Heinkels 111 and Donier 17 in two vics side by side. The enemy aircraft in each vic being smaller vics of three. The bombers were accompanied by a circle of Messerschmitt 109 above them and behind and above that formation there was an echelon of Messerschmitt 110. The Messerschmitt 110 also formed a defensive circle when attacked. Red 1 (F/Lt. Boitel-Gill) and 2 (P/O. Inness) were

36

actually on patrol when informed of the raid, but were unable to contact the rest of the squadron. Yellow 1 (P/O. Cox) and 2 (P/O. Holmes) and White 1 (Sgt. Wolton) and 2 (P/O. Hall) went off together under leadership of Yellow 1. Blue 1 (S/Ldr. Devitt) went off with Blue 2 (Sgt. Holland) and Green 1 (P/O. Williams) and 2 (Sgt. Christie) when enemy aircraft were seen overhead from Warmwell. Black 1 (P/O. Bayles) and 2 (P/O. Marrs) took off after the latter. The squadron was unable to join up in the air. Red 1 who had lost Red 2 followed the enemy formation 10,000 feet above reporting its progress and hoping to join a friendly squadron. As the enemy aircraft approached Bournemouth on its return, Red 1 carried out a frontal quarter attack on a bomber formation of Junkers 88 and when he broke away enemy aircraft was giving out white smoke. It dropped away and then started circling, disappearing below cloud out at sea off Swanage. Red 2 made a frontal attack on the foremost formation of Junkers 88 on three occasions (1) between Portland and Yeovil (2) at Shaftesbury and (3) at Bournemouth, without any effects being seen. Yellow 1 and 2 and White 1 and 2 climbed until they were in front of and above bomber formation and when west of Yeovil delivered frontal attack on the right hand formation of bombers, without any noticeable effect. They became separated. Yellow 1 delivered another head on attack on larger formation of enemy bombers when west of Bristol, but as his machine was hit he returned to Warmwell …

27		When at 1,000 feet, enemy aircraft exploded and crashed south west of Poole Harbour. Black 1 (P/O. Williams) attacked Messerschmitt 110 which after attempting evasive action flew south at full speed. Black 1 continued the attack from astern. The engines of enemy aircraft were pouring out white smoke and dived steeply. Black 1 followed giving short bursts. Enemy aircraft was seen to crash on land between Weymouth and Poole Harbour, near Lulworth Cove. Black 2 (Sgt. Ackroyd) did not intercept any enemy aircraft.
30	16.30	12 Spitfires No. 152 Squadron intercepted formation of 70 Heinkels 111, 30 Messerschmitt 110's and 9 Messerschmitt 109's at 21,000 to 22,000 feet over Portland flying north. The Heinkel 111's were in vics of three in one large vic with

Above: A pair of 152 Squadron Spitfires at readiness by a dispersal hut.
(Author's Collection)

Messerschmitt 110's weaving astern and 1,000 feet above. The squadron was west of Portland, in the sun slightly above the enemy fighters, when they attacked them. After the Squadron formation had been broken up in dog fights, the bombers were also attacked. Red 1 (S/Ldr. Devitt) attacked an Messerschmitt 110 without noticing any effect. He then dived away from the fighters and carried out beam attack on 3 Heinkel 111's in tight vics following into a quarter attack. 2 of the enemy aircraft dropped back both streaming glycol from starboard engine. Red 2 (P/O. Cox) attacked a Messerschmitt 110 giving two bursts from 250 yards closing, bits broke off enemy aircraft. He was then attacked by Messerschmitt 109's, fired at one and went down into clouds. Red 3 (P/O. Bayles) attacked 3 Messerschmitt 110's from forward quarter and they turned head on to him climbed up and attacked from beam and above Heinkel 111 which had dropped out of formation. Enemy aircraft disappeared into cloud. He climbed again and attacked enemy bomber formation when over Warmwell, but without noticeable results. Yellow 1 (P/O. Inness) attacked Messerschmitt 110 from the beam and above, considerable return fire was noticed but no effect from the attack was observed. Yellow 2 (P/O. Hall) lost his section and joined Red section and attacked the bombers. Yellow 3 (Sgt. Sheppherd) attacked the formation of bombers, singled out a Heinkel 111 on which he made an astern attack. He was attacked by 2 Messerschmitt 110 and in return attacked one of them, which he hit at close range and damaged. Blue 1 (F/Lt. Thomas) when about to attack Messerschmitt 110's after Red and Yellow sections had attacked, was attacked by Messerschmitt 109, broke away and lost height failing to contact enemy aircraft again. Blue 2 (Sgt. Ackroyd) followed Blue 1. Blue 3 (P/O. Marrs) attacked bombers from the beam, got in a short burst, received bullet through perspex and in petrol tank from cross fire of bombers. He only got one wheel down and could not get it up again and made excellent landing at Warmwell under difficult circumstances. Green 1 (P/O. Williams) attacked Messerschmitt 110 which went down and to left. He followed it down through the clouds giving long bursts and saw smoke pouring from both engines. When satisfied that enemy aircraft would crash, he climbed again and attacked another Messerschmitt 110 which had one engine pouring white smoke when Hurricane of 56 Squadron broke away. When ammunition of Green 1 failed both engines were pouring smoke, Hurricane attacked again and enemy aircraft went down west of Portland. Green 2 (Sgt. Kearsey) was weaving above Squadron and when it turned to attack he made a surprise attack on Messerschmitt 110 and closed to 50 yards. Enemy aircraft turned over on its back and dived vertically. Green 1 saw this aircraft go down in flames in the vicinity of Chesil Bank or off west end of Fleet. Green 3 (Sgt. Reddington) who was also weaving behind did not return and was posted missing.

OCTOBER
7   15.45   12 Aircraft No. 152 Squadron up from Warmwell 1527 hours intercepted 30 Junkers 88's proceeding N.W. in straggling vics

of three at 17,000 feet. Messerschmitt 110's were behind and 1,000 feet above. The squadron was about 3,000 feet above the Junkers 88's. The Messerschmitt 110's were in line astern and from time to time the leaders of each line turned round and formed a defensive circle. The circle then broke up and Messerschmitt 110's made up with their bombers again. When the squadron intercepted, it went line astern and attacked the bombers after which our formation broke up and dog fights ensued. The bombers turned south between Lyme Regis and Exeter. Messerschmitt 109's were seen after the squadron had attacked the enemy bombers. Red 1 (P/O. Holmes) led the attack on the Junkers 88 from abeam and above breaking downwards and saw no effects although white smoke was seen to be streaming from two bombers after his second attack. He then went up to 23,000 feet and when over Dorchester saw Messerschmitt 109's above him. He lost them when climbing into the sun to attack. Red 2 (P/O. Bayles) after breaking away from attack on bombers without noticing result failed to contact other enemy aircraft. Red 3 (Sgt. Wolton) also failed to intercept enemy aircraft after his attack on bombers. Yellow 1 (Sgt. Sheppherd) when making first attack on 3 Junkers 88 closed to 50 yards. One jettisoned its bombs, began to stream glycol and dropped back. At 4,000 feet it went in to a spin and fell in flames, 4 of the crew baled out. Yellow 2 (P/O. Hall) force-landed at Sutton Scotney near Worthy Down. Yellow 3 (P/O. Cox) attacked vic of 3 Junkers 88's with full deflection closing to the beam damaging one. He then attacked Junkers 88's in vics of 3 and singly. Blue 1 (P/O. Marrs) after attacking Junkers 88's without noticing results, attacked several strings of Messerschmitt 110's in line astern behind the bombers, before they had time to form defensive circles. He got in a burst on last enemy aircraft of one line and one of its engines streamed glycol. He then attacked single Messerschmitt 110, the crew baled out and enemy aircraft dived vertically into the sea. Blue 2 (Sgt. Klein) failed to gain sufficient height as he could not get his oxygen on. Blue 3 (Sgt. Ackroyd) crashed, was severely burnt and was taken to hospital. Green 1 (P/O. Williams) did quarter attack on Junkers 88 giving 8 secs. burst with full deflection, broke away and came up under leading enemy aircraft, firing the remainder of his rounds at it. Green 2 (Sgt. Szlagowski) when about to attack bombers saw 3 Messerschmitt 110's about 3 miles behind him. He climbed into sun and attacked the Messerschmitt 110's firing 3 bursts at close range and broke away. He climbed back into sun and saw white smoke issuing from both engines of enemy aircraft which was losing height. He attacked again and broke away when 2 Messerschmitt 110's were on his tail, landing to refuel at Middle Wallop, then returning to Warmwell. Green 3 (Sgt. Kearsey) when climbing after attack on Junkers 88's was fired at by A.A. and had to lose height again. He continued to search for enemy aircraft but failed to intercept again. When Green 1 was attacking leading Junkers 88 of enemy aircraft formation from below, the Junkers 88's turned just before Yeovil dropping no bombs there. A few minutes later he noticed about 15 Messerschmitt 110's bombing Yeovil from about 16,000 to 17,000 feet. Red 1 noticed that Messerschmitt 109's had a vertical white stripe on the fin. Blue 1 noticed that Messerschmitt 110's were painted white from the nose to the cockpit. R/T was good. No cine guns were carried. There was no appreciable cloud. 9 aircraft landed at Warmwell 1640 hours. 1 landed later.

19   A Red section went on patrol at about 11.00 hours and at a height of 17,000 feet saw a JU.88 at a height of 19,000 feet. Red 1 (F/Lt. Boitel-Gill) ordered line astern, and realising that it would not be possible to climb above the enemy in time to be of use, climbed to deliver a beam attack from below. He fired and closed to 100 yards. He then broke off following at about 1,000 feet below again fired from 300 yards and closing to 50 yards astern and below. Getting to same height as enemy he half rolled on to his back and continued to fire. The hostile aircraft skidded violently as if his starboard engine had cut out. Red 1 then lost sight of hostile aircraft. Red 2 (P/O. Cox) who had watched this attack dived after the JU.88 and fired. The enemy then disappeared into the mist. These incidents commenced over Dorchester and enemy was finally lost 10 miles S.S.W. of Portland. It is considered that the JU.88 was damaged. Our fighters fired approximately 2740 rounds.

20	A very quiet day and no sign of any action taking or likely to be taken against hostile aircraft.
21	There was a certain amount of air activity in the direction of Weymouth and there was a great deal of A.A. fire from there. The Squadron was not warned and when a section did leave the ground the hostile craft, believed to have been two in number, were well out to sea and we had no chance of reaching them. The rest of the day was very quiet. S/Ldr. Devitt proceeded on ten days leave and F/Lt. Boitel-Gill took temporary command. P/O. Heymann (late Captain in the Dorsetshire Regt. retired) took up his appointment as Squadron Adjutant.
22	Another very quiet day and except for routine flights there was "nothing doing". As it might be of interest in the future, herewith the names of the officers of the Squadron, and dates of joining the Squadron.

O.C.	S/Ldr. P.K. Devitt	6/3/40.
	F/Lt. F.M. Thomas	2/10/39.
	F/Lt. B.P.H. Boitel-Gill DFC	12/4/40.
	F/O. R.F. Inness	22/2/40.
	F/Lt. E.S. Hogg	14/11/39.
	P/O. C.S. Cox	1/10/39.
	P/O. T.N. Bayles	24/4/40.
	P/O. F.H. Holmes	22/6/40.
	P/O. G.T. Baynham	5/10/40.
	P/O. R.M.D. Hall	2/9/40.
	P/O. E.S. Marrs	17/3/40.
	P/O. D.W. Williams	18/5/40.
	P/O. D.H. Fox Male	29/9/40.
	P/O. N.E. Hancock	11/10/40.
	P/O. P.H. Humphries	29/9/40.
	P/O. R. Heymann Adjt.	20/10/40.
	P/O. R.H. Davies Eng.	10/10/40.
	P/O. J.M. McBain Intell.	15/5/40.

23	Weather very bad and low cloud. No flying of any importance at all and not the slightest sign of an enemy and not even a warning.
24	Again nothing of interest.
25	Nothing of interest.

26	Nothing of interest. F/Sgt. Hatton who has been F/Sgt. Discipline for some time was posted.
27	While on patrol P/O. Marrs sighted a hostile aircraft but lost it in cloud and never had a chance of getting a "crack" at it.
28	At about 1600 hours the whole Squadron was ordered up, as it was reported that at least fifty enemy planes were on their way to the coast. However, the Squadron landed at about 1730 not having sighted any of the enemy.
29	Nothing to report.
30	Pilot Sgt. Anderson was posted to flying school for further instruction. P/O. E.W. Wootten was posted to the Squadron for duty. Nothing of flying interest.
31	S/Ldr. Devitt returned from leave. P/O. E.W. Wotton's posting cancelled.

SUMMER OF DAPPLED SHADE

The summer of 1940 blazed with a warm and golden glow,
So vanquishing the memory of a cruel winter and suffocate snow.
A band of young men of gladiatorial spirit served us dear at war.
Fighting for our country whilst outnumbered two to the score.

Remember the pilots, who flew their streamlined aeroplanes,
And the service teams with the men who extinguished flames.
Grassy-meadows or farmer-sowed strips always relieving sight,
For men with shattered dials or engines spluttering from a flight.

Our flyers stood fast and firm against swastika-marked marauders,
And smashed and crashed German Messerschmitts and Dorniers.
Yet another scrambled take-off to soar into colossal blue skyways,
As dogfights bloodied and tainted the white cirrus of the highways.

During intervals of peace a few of the Few lounged in deckchairs,
Read books or wrote confidential letters home to allay family fears.
Hundreds of their number died never having flown a victory parade,
But rest neath mature trees born during a summer of dappled shade.

Michael Kendrick
30 December 2003

A formation flypast by 152 Squadron. (Author's Collection)

PART II
The Men of 152 (Hyderabad) Squadron

John and Irene Ackroyd on their wedding day. (Courtesy of Andy Saunders)

ACKROYD, Pilot Officer Harold John
No.86360

Harold Ackroyd was born on 6 September 1913 in Yorkshire and was only a child of 7 when his father died. He was educated at Bishops Wordsworth School, Wiltshire where his mother was a hospital sister at the nearby county hospital. Little else is known of his childhood.

In 1935 he met his future wife Irene: At that time he was living in Ealing, Essex, working with local welfare authorities. More commonly known as John to other squadron pilots, he joined the RAFVR in 1936 as u/t pilot obtaining the number 7400143, carrying out his flying training at 11 FTS Perth. At this stage in his flying career his natural flying ability was evident as he was instructing at a number of training units, attaining the rank of sergeant.

John married Irene in September 1939 and moved to RAF Upavon, followed by RAF Kinloss, Scotland, where they lived in a small farm house close to the airfield. In early 1940 he carried out conversion to Spitfires and was posted to 152 Squadron when it was based at RAF Acklington, with Irene coming to visit him on occasion, staying with her parents for ease. He moved with the squadron to RAF Warmwell and Irene re-joined him in July that year.

On the afternoon of 13 August, having already been in combat that day over Portland he was engaged in heavy fighting with a large formation of enemy aircraft, destroying a Junkers Ju 87. The following action is taken from the Squadron ORB:

> Sgt Ackroyd attacked a Ju 87 and saw his Perspex splinter and the machine went down from formation. He followed it down but was then attacked and his machine was so much damaged and his rudder jammed. He returned to base.

He was flying Spitfire R6910 on this combat engagement. On 25 September, he was commissioned to the rank of pilot officer.

During the afternoon of 7 October John, flying as Blue 3, took off as part of a squadron scramble to intercept a large formation of Ju 88s. They were soon involved in a fierce dog-fight over the Dorset coast. It is believed John was engaged by a Messerschmitt Bf 110 providing escort for the bomber formation. His Spitfire, N3039, caught fire, immediately crashing at Shatcombe Farm, Wynford Eagle, 10 miles west of Dorchester.

Ackroyd was taken to Dorchester Hospital having received serious burns after his aircraft's fuel tank exploded. Irene was duly informed and rushed to be at his side. Sadly, he died the next day of his wounds; Irene remained with him throughout.

A few days later, Sergeant Bill Kearsey's wife saw Irene in Dorchester trying to obtain a refund for his uniforms as they had recently been tailored following his promotion to pilot officer.

John was a very good mechanic and had a great interest in fast sports cars.

He received a full military funeral at Holy Trinity Church, Warmwell. Irene remarried in 1948.

BARKER, Sergeant John Keeth
No.566251

John was born at Birkenhead in 1917. Though little is known of his early life and his education, it can be stated that he joined the RAFVR in 1933, training as a wireless operator with his two friends Eric Shepperd and Ralph Wolton, all three going on to serve together as sergeant pilots in 152 Squadron during the Battle of Britain.

John joined the RAF as an aircraft apprentice in January 1933. He passed out as a wireless operator in December 1935. He subsequently applied for pilot training, eventually joining 152 Squadron direct from 10 FTS on 2 October 1939.

On 18 August 1940, Barker, flying as White 2, with Pilot Officer Graham Cox as White 1, on a patrol at 4,000 feet over the Isle of Wight, claimed his first victory, which he described in his combat report:

> When E/A were sighted (Ju 87) heading south, I dived behind White 1 and attacked Ju 87, to the left of that attacked by White 1. My attack was made from the port upper quarter, opening fire at 200 yards closing to 50 yards with the throttle closed. The E/A, which was about 50 feet above the sea when attacked, dived into the sea at about 30 degrees. I saw no return fire from the rear gunner.

John was in combat again on 25 August, and this time he faced a more fearsome foe:

I was White 2. I sighted a large number of E/A bombers with escorting fighters. In the general melee that resulted, I came down to 8,000ft and climbed up again to 20,000ft into the sun from the E/A. At 20,000ft there were 6 or so lines astern of 7 or 9 109s each, just weaving about.

I joined one of these lines, attacked the last man who rolled onto his back and dived vertically into the sea. At 8,000ft I was again in range and re-opened fire. Putting out smoke and glycol he commenced to pull out at about 5,000ft then steepened and went straight into the sea. The other half of his squadron chased me down, and back to land, but did not hit me.

On 4 September, he failed to return from a sortie. It is believed he was shot down by return fire from a Dornier Do 17, which he engaged twenty-five miles off Bognor Regis in West Sussex. He baled-out but did not survive the fall. His body washed up on the French coast and was buried in Étaples Military Cemetery, France. John was just 23.

Left: Sergeant John Barker's Commonwealth War Graves Commission headstone. (Author's Collection)

BAYLES, Pilot Officer Ian Norman
No.74327

Ian was born on 13 August 1918, in Melbourne, Australia. In 1923 he came to England with his parents and was educated at Winchester and Trinity College, Oxford. He returned to Australia in 1937 but it was decided by his parents he would study law and returned to Oxford with the intention of returning to Melbourne as a qualified lawyer.

While at Oxford he joined the University Air Squadron and transferred to the RAFVR with the number 754313 in June 1939. He was called-up the same year and he completed his training, attaining the rank of pilot officer on 26 September 1939.

Ian joined 152 Squadron on the 20 April 1940 while it was still based at RAF Acklington. At this time, the squadron received its new Spitfires and he was sent to 5 OTU, Aston Down, on 5 May to convert to the aircraft. On 29 May, he was posted to 249 Squadron at RAF Leconfield but, under pressure from Squadron Leader Peter Devitt, he re-joined the squadron on 9 June just before it moved to Warmwell.

The following is taken from the squadron ORB for 13 August:

'P/O Bayles also attacked a Bf 110 and smoke was seen coming from its port engine.'

Ian received the nickname of Dimmy. While the origin of this name is not certain, one pilot stated that Dimmy was the consequence of Ian being a slow mover, perhaps giving 'the impression that he was a bit thick'.

Pilot Officer Roger Hall remembers Ian well when he arrived at the squadron at the end of August:

There was P/O 'Dimmy' who was a red-headed robust sort of person. He had the build you might expect to find in the scrum of a school first fifteen. He gave you the impression of a brute force without much refinement, but he was by no means a crude pilot.

On the contrary, he had excelled himself since the squadron had come down south. He was married, and people thought that this had in some way imposed a newly acquired caution upon him, a caution which before his marriage had not existed. He seemed to be trying to resist an inner conflict, one side which was trying to restrain him and the other, the more natural side, to live and fight as though he had no wish to live forever.

Pilot Officer Dennis Fox-Male described Ian as 'a contemporary of Richard Hillary'. On 25 September, whilst flying as Black 1, Ian was engaged in combat with the enemy over Yeovil, Somerset. He claimed a 'shared' for his part in the destruction of a Heinkel He 111 with three other aircraft, and a probable He 111 destroyed. The He 111 he helped bring down had Hauptmann Helmut Brandt, the Staffelkapitän 6/Kampfgeschwader 55, on board. Brandt was taken prisoner.

Above: Pilot Officer Graham Cox and Pilot Officer Ian Bayles with P/O Pooch. Note the road beacon with a smiley face drawn on. This would have been 'liberated' on one of the squadron's many nights out. (Author's Collection)

Ian was promoted to flying officer on 26 September and the following day was engaged with a number of enemy aircraft from units of Erprobungsgruppe 210 and their Messerschmitt Me 109 fighter escort – once again over the Bristol-Yeovil area. While climbing to engage Me 109s heading backs towards France he was himself engaged by one of the German fighters that had closed in behind him. His port wing was hit by cannon fire and he returned to RAF Warmwell. On his return, an inspection of his aircraft found cannon shell damage in one of his tyres. He damaged a Bf 110 during this engagement.

Due to his operational experience, he would often lead the squadron into combat in the absence of Squadron Leader Peter Devitt or Flight Lieutenant Derek Boitel-Gill. One such occasion was on 7 October. Flying as Red 1, he led the squadron against a large bomber formation. The squadron had the advantage of being 3,000ft above them. The men were given the command to attack by Ian and attacked line astern, breaking up the bomber formation and each taking individual targets. The following is taken from the squadron combat report for Ian's part in the engagement:

> Red 1 led the attack on the Ju 88s from abeam and above breaking downwards and so no effect although white smoke was seen to be streaming from two bombers after his second attack. He then went up to 23,000ft and went over Dorchester, he saw Me 109s above him. He lost them when climbing into the sun to attack. Rounds fired: 1200 1 burst 7 seconds 300-100yds.

Ian was posted away from the squadron on 18 August 1941, to carry out instructional duties. In June 1942, he undertook a gunnery course and was posted to 224 Group, India. On 5 February 1943, he took command of 135 Squadron flying Hurricanes along the Arakan coast. He went on to command 273 Squadron before being promoted to the rank of squadron leader on 30 June 1945 and then appointed wing commander of 902 Wing, receiving the DFC on 2 October 1945. This was to be his last appointment and he returned to the UK to be released from the RAF in July 1946, going back to Australia.

Ian was an important figurehead in the area where he lived in Avenet, Victoria, and was a councillor for seventeen years. He also had a keen interest in horse racing and was on the board of the Victoria Racing Committee for twenty years. His son remembers: 'He was a man of principle, [a] hard task master, but showed great fairness.' He passed away on 12 July 1998.

BAYNHAM, Flying Officer Geoffrey Theodore
No.41518

Geoffrey was born on 15 December 1915 in Dartford, Kent. He was educated at Tonbridge and studied law. Before the war he held a commission in the Territorial Army, serving in the Royal Welsh Regiment, but resigned his commission in 1938. He then enlisted in the RAF, duly completing his pilot training, which commenced on 6 October 1938. During this period he visited Germany and witnessed the inevitable rise of the Nazi Party and the lead up to war.

On 12 September 1939, Geoffrey was posted to 80 Squadron, then based at Amriya, Egypt, flying Gloster Gladiators. While posted there

Above: Flying Officer Geoffrey Baynham. (Courtesy of the Baynham family)

he met Claude Marie Helene Bertrand, the daughter of Victor Bertrand, a French Suez Canal Company official. They were married on 14 February 1940 in the Eglise Saint-Francois de Sales at Ismailia, Egypt.

On his return to the UK in mid-1940 he was posted to 12 OTU at RAF Benson, converting to Fairey Battle light bombers. On completion, he was posted to 4(C) Ferry Squadron on 15 June based at RAF Kemble, then on to the OTU at Hawarden to convert to Spitfires.

Geoffrey was posted to 234 Squadron on 16 September 1940, then based at RAF Middle Wallop. After numerous operational sorties, gaining valuable experience, he was posted to 152 Squadron on 4 October.

An example of the many operational sorties that followed occurred on 28 November. Flying as White 1, at 22,000ft, he was involved in a dogfight with eight other squadron aircraft when Me 109s 'jumped' the squadron. Climbing to engage a lone Me 109, he also witnessed Sergeant Zygmunt Klein being shot down, observing his stricken Spitfire spin from a formation of seven or eight Me 109s.

In March 1941, he was posted back to 234 Squadron, then also at RAF Warmwell. He claimed a Me 109 on 19 May 1941 and a further three Me 109s on 17 July, this second engagement lasting under thirty seconds.

On 17 April 1943, Geoffrey was posted, yet again, to 152 Squadron as a flight commander. At the time the squadron was based at Souk-El-Khemis in North Africa. He was awarded the DFC on 10 September 1943. In 1944 he was posted to RATGROUP – the Rhodesian Air Training Group. While instructing on a course he was involved in a serious night flying accident in a Harvard. The incident resulted in him being hospitalised for a long period at Salisbury and Johannesburg suffering from head injuries. Indeed, so serious were his injuries that this accident ending his flying career. He retired from the RAF with the rank of flight lieutenant.

After the war, Geoffrey divorced. Remaining in the UK, he re-married in 1947, but decided to move back to Southern Rhodesia, a country that had captivated him during his time there. Buying a Percival Proctor aircraft, and despite having no radio communication equipment on board, he flew back there with his second wife.

Due to the political situation in Rhodesia, in time the couple moved to South Africa. Suffering from cancer, Geoffrey passed away on 1 May 1990. His ashes were scattered on Table Top Mountain.

Above: Geoffrey and Claude Marie Helene Bertrand on their wedding day. (Courtesy of the Baynham family)

BEAUMONT, Pilot Officer Walter
No.76308

Walter was born on 21 June 1914, in Wakefield, Yorkshire. He was educated at Hebden Bridge Grammar School and went on to be awarded a BSc in science from the University of London. He trained to become a science teacher, taking up a post at Enfield Grammar School, Middlesex, where he was also a training instructor.

Walter joined the RAFVR in 1937, gaining the service number 740000, which indicates he was the first person to join the RAFVR. He moved to Coulsdon, Surrey, with his wife. He was living there when he was called-up for full-time service on the outbreak of war.

Commissioned on 10 December 1939, he was posted to 152 Squadron while it was based at RAF Acklington. He moved to RAF Warmwell with the squadron and was soon involved in combat engagements over the South Coast.

Pilot Officer Walter Beaumont relaxing at home in his family garden.
(Courtesy of the Beaumont family)

On 8 August, while flying Spitfire R6811 as Green 2, he was part of a force of nine squadron aircraft vectored to patrol at 15,000ft over the infamous Convoy *Peewit* – this was moving down the English Channel close to Portland Harbour. As soon as the squadron took-off from Warmwell it entered thick cloud and the aircraft soon lost each other. Walter, with Flying Officer Edward Hogg as Green 1, steadied out at 12,000ft and began the patrol. They were suddenly attacked by twenty plus Me 109s that had pounced from above out of the sun. The following is an extract from the squadron combat report for this engagement:

> Green 2 after seeing a large number of Me 109s at 3,000ft above saw 12 Me 109s coming down. After calling up Blue leader to inform him, he turned to meet the Me 109s but could not climb fast enough. They passed overhead onto the tail of the formation. He turned back and saw Black 2 attacked and go down vertically trailing black smoke. He turned to face several more Me 109s coming down on his tail and lost his formation. He went up in a steep climbing turns dodging the E/A.
>
> While still climbing he attacked a Me 109 tail attack with slight deflection, ½ second burst, but saw Me 109 coming on his tail from above and behind to his left. He did a steep turn to the left and immediately received fire from Me 109. The cockpit filled with smoke and Green 2 went down out of control and force-landed. Rounds fired: one burst ½ second.

Walter successfully force-landed his Spitfire at Spyway Farm, Langton Matravers. He was promptly taken to the nearest public house where, on his arrival, he was surprised to encounter Sergeant Denis Robinson. Flying as Black 2, Denis had been shot down during the same engagement. Hauptmann Gunther von Maltzahn and Hauptmann Heinz Bretnutz, both of 2/Jagdgeschwader 53, were the Me 109 pilots who engaged and shot down Walter and Denis during this combat.

On 12 August, the squadron encountered a large enemy formation, consisting of Ju 88s with fighter protection over the Isle of Wight. Flying at an altitude of between 2,000ft and 3,000ft, Walter, again flying as Green 2 and accompanied by Blue 1 and Blue 2, attacked a Ju 88, which they believed they had damaged. He pulled away and went in again, this time with Green 1, Flying Officer Edward Hogg, and attacked

Pilot Officer Walter Beaumont (Author's Collection)

another Ju 88. The latter was last seen emitting black smoke, after pieces had fallen off it.

The very next day, Walter attacked a Me 110, but quickly another Me 110 got on his tail. He dropped his aircraft into a steep dive and successfully escaped his purser. He re-entered the fray and attacked another Me 110, which turned on its back and dived vertically into cloud.

His second confirmed engagement was on 16 August 1940, when the squadron was on patrol over the Isle of Wight. Flying at 20,000ft 5 miles off Ventnor, a large formation of Me 110s with a fighter escort of Me 109s were spotted. Evasive action was taken and both sides soon become locked together in battle. The action was so rapid that no pilot had the chance of immediately opening fire or visualising the field of combat. However, Walter managed to pull away and attacked three Me 109s, shooting two of them down.

Two days later, on 18 August, while flying as Blue 1, Walter was part of eleven aircraft to be engaged in aerial combat, over Portsmouth at 4,000ft, with a formation of Ju 87s and Me 109s, the latter acting as

The wreckage of Obergefreiter Willi Kuhweide's Junkers Ju 88. (Author's Collection)

fighter protection. The squadron dived on the Ju 87s, attacking in line astern. Walter went in to attack a group of scattered Ju 87s:

> Blue 1 attacked a Ju 87 and he saw its wheels touch the water and bounce out. The leader saw this a/c dive into the sea. Blue 1 attacked another Ju 87 from above; fired a 4 second burst and the a/c dived straight into the sea. Blue 1 saw a Ju87 shot down in flames by Blue 2. He also saw White 1's engaging a Me 109 which was streaming oil from White 1's burst. After break away he saw Me109 tail sticking out of the sea.

Walter's next victim was a Ju 88A-1 on 22 August. This aircraft, 7A+AL of 3 Staffel, Fernaufklarungsgruppe 121, had been carrying out a reconnaissance of RAF Filton when it was engaged by Green Section. It crashed into a field of marigolds at Upcott Farm, Beaford near Okehampton, Devon, at 16.00 hours. The farm was owned by a gentleman farmer, Mr Putticombe. Sheila Tredinnick's father was working in the fields as a farm labourer when he witnessed the crash:

> On hearing the crash the farm hands, one of whom was my father, rushed to the scene with pitch forks in hand, to see what could be done. On investigation, it was clear the pilot was dead. With the contempt for the German people at the time, it was suggested that the pilot be removed from the wreckage and disposed of in a pit to be dug close by.
>
> Before the work could be completed, Mr Putticome arrived on the scene and was horrified at what the men planned to do, and rebuked them, saying: 'Whether a German or not, that man is some-one's son. He will have a proper Christian burial, the same as any of you would expect'. Although very young, I remember my father frequently relating the incident.

The aircraft crashed with its starboard engine on fire and soon burned out. The crew comprised Obergefreiter Willi Kuhweide (killed), Leutnant Reinhard Pfundtner (PoW, injured), Oberleutnant Rudolf Baudler (PoW, injured), and Flieger Anton Leber (PoW, injured).

Three days later, on 25 August, he had a 'shared' Me 109, an E-1, White 15, of Jagdgeschwader 53. It came down at Tatton House Farm, Buckland Ripers, Dorset, at 17.30 hours. The other RAF pilots involved in the combat were Pilot Officer R.P. Beaumont, 87 Squadron, and Sergeant R.T. Llewellyn, 213 Squadron. The Luftwaffe pilot, Gefreiter Josef Brocker, later recounted what happened:

> In the morning, I/JG53 had flown from Rennes to the operational airfield near Cherbourg. I was not due to fly that day but because one pilot from our Staffel could not get his plane to start I ended up flying. After receiving our orders, we went to our planes. I flew the one marked '15' and as I was the most inexperienced pilot (I had come to the frontline in early August). I had to fly as Katschmarek to my Staffel Kapitaen. Hauptmann Mayer, behind me flew two experienced comrades.
>
> Below us I could see the bombers (Ju 88s) and their escort. We had to fly a Freie Jagd mission. It was an emotional feeling to see, all of a sudden, the English coast beneath us. The sky was blue, no cloud to give us protection in case of emergency.
>
> Our Staffel Kapitaen had noticed enemy fighters and ordered us to attack. However, it was Spitfires that attacked us, coming out of the sun. Both near and far there were dogfights. We attacked the Spitfires by turning left and the Staffel Kapitaen fired the fire bursts and I followed him. Both comrades behind me broke away and had their own dogfights.
>
> Suddenly I felt my plane being hit; it climbed for a moment lost speed and inverted dived away. I got into a spin to the left and there was no feeling to the control column. I saw the view of England, France, England but I could not regain control. There was another hit to my plane and I noticed some pressure on my control column. I tried to get out of the spin, I pulled out of the dive towards the Channel and I noticed that I was at an altitude of 1,000m. I supposed the engine had been hit; the airscrew was just wind-milling and was then engaged by three or possibly four more British fighters which cut of my retreat. I lost more and more height and looked for a landing place. By this time the British fighters were lining up behind me so there was no chance of escaping.
>
> I landed in a field and after I had regained my calmness I set fire to my plane. I had put my silk scarf into the fuel injection pump and lit it with a match. The plane exploded and I suffered burns to my hand and face. I also suffered spinal strain because of the force-landing.

Above: Gefreiter Josef Brocker. (Courtesy of Chris Goss)

Below: Gefreiter Josef Brocker's Bf 109. (Courtesy of Chris Goss)

Two men approached me and said 'Good day sir, how are you?' At this moment, I realised that I was taken as a PoW. They both took me to a house where I received first aid. Shortly afterwards soldiers appeared who took me back to my burnt-out plane which by now was almost completely burnt out. From there they brought me to an airfield which had obviously just been attacked by the Ju 88s. Little did I realise that from this time onwards I would stay in British and Canadian captivity until 7 January 1947 when I was released and could go home.[1]

His tally continued to mount, the next being a 'shared' He 111 on 27 August. On this day he was hit by return fire from a Ju 88 and he had to bale-out of his Spitfire, R6831, which crashed into the Channel 8 miles off Portland. He also claimed a 'damaged' Do 215 on 7 September.

Walter had been in almost constant combat for nearly two months. After a combat on 23 September, he did not return to Warmwell. Neither his body nor his Spitfire, R7016, were ever found. It is believed that he was not meant to be flying that day as he had been grounded due to fatigue and was due to be posted to a training squadron. He was 26-years-old at the time of his death.

For having successfully engaged eleven aircraft, destroying eight and damaging three, Walter was posthumously awarded the DFC on 22 October 1940. The announcement in *The London Gazette* states, 'this officer has displayed great skill and determination in air combat against the enemy and had destroyed six of their aircraft'.

Walter Beaumont's strong self-belief is succinctly portrayed by a comment he made in a letter he wrote to his parents: 'We Beaumonts' can make success from anything we tackle.'

BOITEL-GILL, Flight Lieutenant Derek Pierre Aumale No.28142

Derek was born on 23 March 1911 at Thames Ditton. He was educated at Milbourn Lodge School and Steyne School, Worthing.

Derek joined the RAF in September 1929, being commissioned on the 13th of the same month. He was duly posted to 5 FTS, Sealand, to undertake his initial training. He was then posted to 3 Squadron at RAF Upavon on 9 September 1940. He remained there until he joined the list

Above: Flight Lieutenant Derek Boitel-Gill outside dispersal. (Author's Collection)

in 1934. During this time, he became the personal pilot to the Nizam of Hyderabad. He also flew for Imperial Airways.

In early 1940, Derek was re-called to the RAF due to a shortage of pilots in Fighter Command. He joined 152 (Hyderabad) Squadron while it was still at RAF Acklington: It is not known if he was posted to this squadron due to having been the Nizam's personal pilot.

He was promoted to the rank of Flight Lieutenant on 22 April 1940. He undertook escort duties and normal sorties with the rest of the squadron until 5 May, when he was posted to 5 OTU, Aston Down. There he converted to Spitfires, remaining there as an instructor. He became one of the senior instructors teaching pilots to fly the Boulton Paul Defiant.

Derek, who came to be known by the nickname 'Bottle', from his lengthy surname, was posted back to 152 Squadron on 27 July 1940, by which time had it moved to Warmwell. On his return, he took command of 'A' Flight.

Above: Cuthbert Orde's drawing of Flight Lieutenant Derek Boitel-Gill DFC.
(Author)

On 11 August, while flying at 17,000ft over Portland, the squadron was intercepted by a force of Me 109s. The RAF pilots took evasive action with the command of 'break' being yelled over the R/T. Flying as Yellow 1 and climbing in height, he spotted enemy fighters above and in front of him. He fired two short bursts at 500 yards and, closing the range to 200 yards, continued to engage the enemy aircraft – but with no effect.

His first confirmed 'kill' occurred on 12 August when he was engaged in heavy fighting over St Catherine's Point. The raiders on this occasion consisted of a large formation of Ju 88s with fighter escort being provided by Me 109s and Me 110s. The Ju 88s were formed-up ready to attack the RDF station below them. The squadron attacked in line astern. A fierce combat ensued, during which Derek was flying as Blue 2. The following is taken from the squadron combat report:

> Blue 2 followed a Junkers 88 in a dive and attacked it from above, when it pulled out. E/A burst into flames immediately.
>
> Green 1 and 2 followed Blue section, each attacked different Junkers 88s which they damaged. They then did a combined attack on a Junkers 88 which was last seen emitting black smoke, after pieces had fallen off it. Rounds fired: 1352.

His next engagement came the following day, 13 August, when he led the squadron in an attack on a formation of thirty Me 110s. No damage was caused to the enemy. He then spotted another large formation over Portland, this one consisting of Ju 87s with a fighter escort of Me 109s and Me 110s. The Spitfires dived on the German aircraft. Derek observed his rounds hit home into the fuselage of one Ju 87. The aircraft broke up instantly in the air. He then singled out a pair of Me 110s, shooting them both down in succession. While attacking these aircraft, they both returned fire, seriously damaging his own aircraft.

With many cannon holes in his fuselage and losing glycol, he returned towards home. As the ORB states for this engagement: 'His machine was extremely badly damaged; him bringing it back to base was undoubtedly a magnificent effort.'

The Ju 87B he attacked was flown by Feldwebel Linderschmid and Gefreiter Eisold. It crashed between Portesham and Rodden, Dorset, at 16.00 hours. The following is an account from a local man who witnessed this engagement:

Above: Flight Lieutenant Derek Boitel-Gill. (Author's Collection)

Above: Civilians removing wreckage from the crash site of Feldwebel Linderschmid. (Author's Collection)

My neighbours and I had been watching an aerial battle and machine-gun ammunition clips had fluttered down around us. Suddenly there was a bloodcurdling banshee wail. It was heart stopping as it approached us.

Right over our heads came the stricken 'plane. There was dense black smoke pouring from its starboard engine and the two young airmen were clearly visible. They had just seconds to live. Later came the news that a German 'plane had crashed behind Grimstone Viaduct. We went there immediately on our bikes but a sentry was there on guard with fixed bayonet. Beneath two white parachutes were the crumpled bodies of the airmen.

The two airmen were interred in a green unploughed curve at the side of the field as it was believed the local vicar refused to perform a burial service in his churchyard. They were eventually re-interred in their home country of Germany in the 1960s.

At around the middle of August, Pilot Officer Roger Hall arrived at the squadron. One of the first people he met was Derek, who would

Above: The grave of Feldwebel Linderschmid and Gefreiter Eisold, in a hedge row, marked by a wooden cross. (Author's Collection)

become his flight commander: 'Bottle was a tall and slender sort of person and eminently refined in his speech, appearance and behaviour. Everything he did was precise and his skill in the air was second to none.'

On 18 August whilst leading the squadron in an attack against an enemy formation of an estimated thirty Ju 87s with fighter protection from Me 109s, which was attacking the CH radar station at Ventnor on the Isle of Wight. The squadron was flying at 4,000ft when the enemy was spotted 4 miles from land. Flying as Red 1, Boitel-Gill gave the command 'Tally Ho!', this being the signal for the squadron to attack in line astern:

> Red 1 attacked a Ju 87 and after a short burst E/A went into the sea. Red 1 also attacked another three other E/A. One of which appeared to get into difficulty. He did not see this E/A hit the water. The other two E/A probably damaged. Red 1 was himself attacked by E/A. The Ju 87s were coloured dark green and the Me 109s were coloured a lighter blue than usual. The latter being a most effective camouflage.

Derek was a keen smoker and always carried with him a cigarette case which would only hold two cigarettes. His habit was once remarked upon by Pilot Officer Roger Hall: 'If it had been possible to smoke [in the air] I'm sure that bottle would have been puffing away contently, elegantly tapping the ash from a cigarette held in its holder into some convenient receptacle probably the map-case. Such composure that I don't suppose he would have bothered to remove the cigarette from his mouth even during a dog-fight with half a dozen Me 109s.'

When he had the chance to relax he would visit friends in Bournemouth, often taking other members of his flight with him. One of the hosts, who was named Pam, would help the pilots relax by pouring them a drink and then to simply sit and listen, or talk, to them.

On 25 September, a large formation of enemy aircraft was spotted over Portland. Already in the air over RAF Warmwell flying as Red 1, observing the formation of aircraft he attempted to contact Control to warn them of the raid – but without success. Nevertheless, by the time the enemy formation was over the airfield the remainder of the squadron had taken-off.

As the Spitfire pilots did not have the chance to form up as a squadron, and were therefore forced to work in pairs or alone, it was a case of every pilot for himself:

> Red 1, who had lost Red 2, followed the enemy bombers 10,000ft above reporting its progress and hoping to join a friendly Squadron. As E/A approached Bournemouth on its return. Red 1 carried out a frontal quarter attack on a bomber formation of Ju88s. And when he broke away an E/A was giving out white smoke. It dropped away and then started circling, disappearing below cloud out at sea off Swanage.

That same afternoon he was again commanding the aircraft of 'A' Flight on a routine patrol over Portland when they were vectored by Control to locate three possible enemy aircraft. Moving into a 'search' formation they began searching for the raiders. It was Derek who spotted Me 109s closing fast from behind on a member of his Flight. One Me 109 fired at the Spitfire only for the trio to then break away and dive into clouds. Derek followed them down, his attitude dropping to 1000ft. When the Me 109s came within range he fired a short burst hitting the rear aircraft.

Smoke began to pour from the Me 109 and it went into a steep dive through more cloud, finally crashing into the sea.

Pilot Officer Dennis Fox-Male recalled the 'A' Flight leader: 'Bottle was the same age as Peter Devitt I think. He was slim, slightly bald, always with a cigarette in a holder when on the ground, always keen for a beer with the boys and had a capacity which then outstripped them. A brilliant cool pilot and excellent shot.'

On 26 September, he was again leading the squadron, flying as Red 1, when nine of 152 Squadron's aircraft engaged an estimated thirty Ju 88s, the latter being escorted by the omnipresent gaggle of Me 109s. Red Section attacked a formation of Ju 88s in line astern formation. After a second attack, both times approaching from the sun, three enemy aircraft were observed to drop out of their formation. One crashed on the Isle of Wight, the other two fell into the sea 7 miles off the Isle of Wight.

On 19 October he attacked a lone Ju 88 over Dorchester at 19,000ft. with his No.2, Pilot Officer Graham Cox, who was flying as Red 2. Both attacked from below and starboard. He broke off his attack, coming back in for a second pass. This time he knocked out the raider's starboard engine. Red 2, likewise, went in for his attack and continued to fire his guns until the Ju 88, now over the sea, entered into a slow spin. Its port wing was seen to break away and fall into the water, at which point two of the enemy crew baled-out of their stricken aircraft. One airman's parachute did not deploy correctly and he fell from the sky, hitting the water close to the wreck of his aircraft.

At the moment he had observed the bomber's wing break away, Derek was heard to remark on the R/T: 'I don't think he will get home like that.'

Derek was awarded the Distinguished Flying Cross on 22 October 1940, the same day as Pilot Officer Walter Beaumont. The announcement in *The London Gazette* states:

> In August 1940, this officer, as leader of his Squadron intercepted an enemy formation consisting of thirty bombers which were escorted by some ninety fighters. As a result of his skills leadership five of the enemy aircraft were destroyed, of which number Flight Lieutenant Boitel-Gill destroyed three. A further three enemy aircraft were damaged in the conflict. On a previous occasion Flight Lieutenant Boitel-Gill destroyed a Ju 88.

Personnel from JG2 pictured in France during 1940. (Courtesy of Andy Saunders)

Sergeant Denis Robinson remembered making a comment about tactics in front of Derek on one occasion. Robinson had found himself flying 'tail end Charlie' far more than what he considered his fair share. Robinson put this down both to upsetting his superiors and being an NCO.

Having been promoted to squadron leader on 1 December 1940, he took command of the squadron. He fulfilled this role until he was posted to 59 OTU at Crosby-on Eden, as wing commander flying, on 17 June 1941.

Derek was killed just a few weeks later. On 18 September, he was demonstrating to a class of trainee pilots the art of 'strafing' enemy ground targets. The 'target' was a concrete pillbox on the edge of the airfield. What happened was recounted by Pilot Officer Dennis Fox-Male in his diary (the following entry being quoted from the Battle of Britain London Monument website):

> He was giving practice to the gunners on the gun posts round the airfield – a daily duty which we took in turn. Cloud base was about 600 to 800 feet. He was diving on the gun posts, flying low on the runway then climbing up into the cloud where he did a stall turn and came down in a dive again.
>
> The dive was steep and he flattened out at about 5 or 6 feet above the ground but poor Bottle forgot that a Hurricane still sinks after the stick is pulled back hurriedly even if it is in a level or even climbing position. A Spitfire never behaved in this way, but Bottle left his pull out too late, the Hurricane sank and hit the ground. He was thrown out and killed.

Aged 30 at the time of his death, Wing Commander Boitel-Gill was cremated at West Norwood Crematorium, London, where he is commemorated on a memorial wall.

CHRISTIE, Sergeant John McBean
No.741898

John was born in Glasgow on 23 August 1918, and lived with his parents in Oldhall, Paisley, Renfrewshire. Little is known of his education. He joined the RAFVR as a u/t pilot, and was called up for full-time service on the outbreak of war. Before war was declared he

Above: Sergeant John McBean Christie standing next to UM-N. (Author's Collection)

---

had met a young lady, also from Paisley, called Williamina. He proposed to her on Christmas Day 1939. She followed him into the RAF and soon joined the WAAF.

'Jack', as he was nicknamed, carried out his flying training at 10 FTS, Tern Hill, from 5 November 1939 until early May 1940. He converted to Spitfires at 7 OTU, Hawarden, and joined 152 Squadron in August of the same year.

There are only a few mentions of John flying during operations. One of these engagements was on 7 September, when he was flying as Green 2:

> 2 a/c Green Section, P/O Beaumont and Sgt Christie when at 20,000ft over Lyme Regis saw a Do 215 10 miles out to sea going south. The section gave chase. The Dornier dived to sea level and the section attacked 10 miles south of Portland. Green 2 was only able to give one short burst from astern as the e/a was so near the sea that he had to break away.

While in combat on 25 September, flying again as Green 2, he dived on a Ju 88 with such speed and force that he blacked-out, only regaining consciousness a few hundred feet from the ground.

On 26 September, he took-off with eight other aircraft to intercept an enemy force of roughly thirty Ju 88s and escorting Me 109s which was flying over the Isle of Wight at 14,000ft. As 'B' Flight went in on the rearmost section of enemy bombers, the escorting Me 109s counter-attacked.

John was hit instantly by cannon fire. His Spitfire K9882 crashed into the sea off Swanage at 16.50 hours. He was picked up by a rescue launch from 30 ASR based at RAF Calshot, Gosport and Cowes, but pronounced dead at the scene. He was 22 years-old and was buried at Arkleston Cemetery, Renfrewshire.

Above: Sergeant Christie with Williamina, his fiancée. (Courtesy of Williamina's family)

COX, Pilot Officer Graham James No.41668

Graham was born on 3 March 1919 in Sparkhill, Birmingham. He was educated at Manly Hall College and Solihull School. He joined the RAF on a short service commission in January 1939. After completing his training and conversion to Spitfires, he was posted to 152 Squadron in early 1940. He moved with the squadron from RAF Acklington to RAF Warmwell on 11-12 July 1940, and was soon given the nickname 'Cocky' Cox.

On 20 July, while returning from a combat sortie while on patrol over Convoy *Bosom* flying Spitfire K9883, a tyre burst and his undercarriage collapsed. He skidded across the airfield before safely coming to a stop unhurt.

On 12 August, flying as Yellow 1, Graham took-off as part of a squadron scramble to intercept a large formation of enemy aircraft over St Catherine's Point. The squadron dived on the enemy aircraft, a large number of Ju 88s, Me 110s and Me 109s, the individual pilots singling out their own targets. Graham and his No.2, Pilot Officer Richard Hogg, carried out an attack on a Ju 88. It states in the squadron combat report for this engagement: 'Yellow 1 and 2 attacked a Ju 88 which landed on sea 20 miles S.E of Sandown. Rounds fired: 2,500.' Graham was duly given a 'shared'.

Pilot Officer Roger Hall remembers him well:

> Cocky was a tall fair-haired pilot of about the same age as I was. He had been in the squadron since it was formed at Acklington earlier in the year and had seen some action on a small scale up in Northumberland before coming south to Warmwell, our present airfield.
>
> Cocky was a veteran. He was a very friendly sort of person and sensitive enough to gauge the uneasiness of others who felt not quite at home, such as me. He was a complete extrovert. He would always be ragging like an overgrown schoolboy and he had an apparently inexhaustible supply of energy. He was conscientious and thorough to the point of fanaticism in the air. If there were ever the remotest chance of intercepting a bandit, even in total darkness, Cocky would always have a go.

Pilot Officer Dennis Fox-Male also had fond memories of Graham:

> Graham was a Cherubic young pilot, one of the bravest who did not have a great deal of luck with 152. He was a great joker, enjoyed vast quantities of beer and was always at the centre of any squadron party.
>
> I remember the squadron throwing a party for the officers at the Grand Hotel, Swange. As a matter of courtesy some of the Air Gunnery School Officers were also invited along with wives and girlfriends of 152 officers. It was to celebrate the 65th victory of the squadron, it was the first anniversary of the formation of the squadron and the party was given and paid for by the Nizam of

Pilot Officer Graham Cox. (Courtesy of the Cox family)

Hyderabad. It was a great success and the pilots managed to get back the 20-odd miles in the early morning, some to go straight to dispersal and snatch a few hours' sleep before dawn readiness.

After breakfast the next morning I happened to pass Cocky's large brown car in the car park of the officers' mess and saw a girl in a black evening dress fast asleep in the back. By lunch time she had disappeared and I never did discover who she was or how he got her away from Warmwell.

On 13 August, he damaged a Me 110, which was last seen turning on its back and diving vertically into cloud. With its fate uncertain, Graham was credited a 'damaged'.

On 18 August, flying as White 1, Graham, with the rest of the squadron, engaged a large enemy formation over Portsmouth:

White 1 half rolled onto a Ju 87 fired a short burst closing to point blank and broke too left and up. But saw no apparent damage. He then fired at other Ju 87s and at Me 109s. He attacked Me 109 which was on Spitfires tail. This E/A was also attacked by Blue 1 and went into the sea.

He saw 4 Me 109s flying low across the Isle of Wight and fired one short burst at E/A at 50yds but with no apparent result. As his ammunition was finished he returned home.

As the battle raged, on 21 August, Graham, flying as part of Red Section, took-off for a routine patrol at 6,000ft over Swanage. A lone Ju 88, seemingly returning to France, was soon spotted. Graham's section immediately attack the enemy bomber, carrying out a No.1 attack in line astern formation. The bomber was seen to emit white smoke and began losing height. After a minute and a half, it crashed into the sea.

Graham was very much a family man and when on leave would return home to his family in the Midlands. On one occasion he was travelling with his father in the family car when his father started complaining about the lack of road signs, these, of course, having been removed in the summer of 1940 due to the threat of invasion. Graham turned to him and replied: 'Pop, there are no sign posts up in the sky.' His father did not complain any more.

The reality was that there was little opportunity for fighter pilots to take leave during the Battle of Britain. On 27 September, when in action

Another picture of Pilot Officer Graham Cox. (Courtesy of the Cox family)

against a large enemy formation of bombers which, with heavy fighter protection, had been heading towards the Dorset coast. Flying as Yellow 1 he destroyed a Me 110.

On 30 September, he claimed a Me 110 'damaged' south of Yeovil. On 7 October, flying as Yellow 3, he was engaged in aerial combat against a large enemy formation of Ju 88s with a fighter escort of Me 110s and Me 109s. A fierce dogfight occurred: 'Yellow 3 attacked vic of 3 Ju 88s with full deflection, closing to the beam damaging one. He attacked Ju 88s in vics of 3 and singly. Rounds fired: 2,800 7 short bursts 200yds-350yds.'

During combat over Portland, Graham blacked-out in a tight turn and his aircraft began to go into a vertical spin. He regained consciousness and heaved back on the controls, eventually taking back control of his aircraft. But due to the G-force the seat attachments broke and the seat fell forward on to the elevator controls. He had to land back at the airfield standing on his rudder pedals.

A member of the squadron's ground-crew, Leading Aircraftman 2nd Class Alf Allsop, was on duty at RAF Warmwell that day. He recalled watching the aircraft returning:

> We saw this Spit coming into land but it would pitch nose up then nose down. Something was wrong and we ran over to it as it landed. The hood went back and Cocky leapt out and was sick on the grass beside the plane.
>
> The seat had busted during a pull out and was resting on the control runs, hence the jerky motion of the plane. He'd had to try to stand up just to move the stick. He was a big lad and a Spit cockpit was a tight fit for anyone. Don't know how he did it.

On 19 October, Graham claimed a 'shared' kill of a Ju 88 over Dorchester, the other pilot involved being Flight Lieutenant Boitel-Gill.

Sergeant Bill Kearsey remembers Graham well, and served with him throughout the Battle of Britain and into 1941:

> Ah! Dear old Cocky, he didn't give a bugger. He ran his car on 100 Octane, quite illegal. But the car wasn't taxed or insured either. I remember seeing it weaving wildly down the front at Weymouth. The driver waving his arms and yelling, 'The steering has gone! Keep clear, keep clear.' Cocky was down on his knees out of sight

Pilot Officer Graham Cox enjoying Weymouth's beach. (Author's Collection)

Outside dispersal having just returned from a combat sortie. This photograph illustrates Graham's character. (Author's Collection)

driving it. It was going to fast too. I am sure he couldn't see properly.

One night coming out of a pub they spotted a barrel of beer in a passage and they picked it up and popped it in the back of his car. Very welcome later. Sometimes I half expected a rocket in the morning after one of these stunts but people gave us a lot of leeway.

One thing that did bother Cocky was one morning he came in looking glum and said to me. 'Bill, I've got to go to the dentist.' I said 'okay see you later', he said, 'I hate going to the dentist.'

'Well nor me likes it Cocky.' And then it was, 'Come with me Bill', 'What!' Oh! go on Bill, be a Sport'. So off we went to the dentist, good old Cocky.

Graham was posted in 1941 after a very successful career with the squadron. Bill Kearsey believes this posting was due to the local constabulary becoming increasingly interested in Graham's large Humber car.

Having claimed a further eight enemy aircraft damaged or

Pilot Officer Graham Cox. (Courtesy of the Cox family)

destroyed while serving with various other squadrons, Cox was awarded the Distinguished Flying Cross on 17 October 1941. He went on to become a flight commander with Nos. 43 and 501 squadrons, serving in Tunisia and Malta. He was promoted to squadron leader, taking command of 229 Squadron, and then 92 Squadron in February 1944, the latter being stationed at Marcianise, Italy.

On 10 October 1944, Graham was awarded the Distinguished Service Order. He retired from the RAF in 1946.

Maintaining his links with India, Graham went on to fly for the Maharaja of Bixanier. In 1951 he emigrated to Calgary in Alberta, Canada, where he began a successful career with Mobil Oil.

Tragedy struck in March 1968 when Graham was involved in an aeroplane crash in Alaska, when the aircraft he was in was brought down by bad weather. Rescue aircraft and ground parties found it extremely difficult to locate the wreckage. When, after four days, they succeeded, it was found that all of the crew and passengers had died of hypothermia.

He was undoubtedly one of the most respected pilots of the squadron during the Battle of Britain and when its former members learned of his death they were deeply saddened. In a letter sent to Graham's family, Flying Officer Edward Deanesly (see the following biography) remarked: 'I grew to admire increasingly his skill as a fighter pilot. He was always irrepressibly cheerful and very good company.' His family commented: 'He was loved dearly by his family; The best! Everyone loved Graham, he had a great personality; he was one of nature's greats!'

DEANESLY, Flying Officer Edward Christopher
No.90251

Edward Deanesly was born on 7 January 1910 in Wolverhampton. He was educated at Wellington College. After his schooling, he went to work in the family business at the Sunbeam factory close to the family home in Wolverhampton.

He joined 605 Squadron Auxiliary Air Force in 1937, being commissioned on 18 March that year. He had a flying accident on 21 June while flying Avro Tutor X3759, when he crash-landed at Pipe Hayes, Birmingham, the aircraft receiving severe damage.

On the outbreak of the Second World War, Christopher, as he was preferred to be known, was called-up for regular service on 24 August

Flying Officer Christopher 'Jumbo' Deanesly. (Courtesy of the Deanesly family)

1939, being posted to 152 Squadron on its reformation on 1 October 1939. The squadron was then stationed at RAF Acklington.

One evening Christopher was flying Gloster Gladiator N2306 on a night navigation exercise. The aircraft began to have engine difficulties and he decided it would be safer to land at the nearest airfield. He touched-down at Eastleigh, landing successfully.

He moved with the squadron to RAF Warmwell on 11-12 July 1940, practising formation flying and making use of the target practice facilities that were then available at the airfield. Christopher once recalled an occasion when, while in charge of a detachment of Gladiators from 152 Squadron, he was 'very rashly let loose on a Spitfire' – this being the first time he had flown the type.

On 25 July, while flying Spitfire K9901, with the rest of the squadron he engaged a large formation of Ju 87s, Me 109s and one Do 17 bomber. On this occasion he was flying as Yellow 1, with Pilot Officer Richard Hogg as Yellow 2: 'F/O Deanesly … attacked a Do 17 (No.1 attack). Cannon fire was experienced from the rear gun.'

After the attack on the lone Do 17, Deanesly spotted a swarm of Ju 87s attacking shipping below. The following is his personal account of this engagement:

> I followed down hard and could see bombs dropping around me as I got nearer the ship. I shot at two bombers on the way down and then flattened out and went after another escaping rapidly away. I easily caught him and finished my ammunition with a long steady burst.
>
> I noticed him firing at me and shortly after the cockpit filled with black smoke. I had difficulty in seeing my compass but after a slight delay I headed north and climbed to 3,000ft. I then realised my glycol had gone and the engine was not going to last long. I hoped to make land but at 1,000ft I decided this was impossible so I called up the control by radio and gave my approximate position. I had left it too late to bail [sic] out so I loosened the straps and made sure my oxygen tub was free and opened the cockpit door. As we glided down at approximately 120mph I crouched with my feet on the seat and as we touched the sea I pulled the control column back and kicked clear, as I knew the chance of coming up if I went down with the aircraft to be small.

I next remember being in the sea quite comfortable not at all distressed having shed my parachute and shoes. The sea was calm and warm and there was no sign of the aircraft.

Among the many vessels below this unfolding drama was the SS *Empire Henchman*, which was towing a lighter loaded with ammunition bound for Falmouth. The steamer's crew watched Christopher land his aircraft on the water and quickly came to his rescue. He remembers the sight of this vessel: 'I looked around and saw a ship's smoke on the horizon. A Hurricane flying low spotted me, circled around and directed the ship towards me.'

From the SS *Empire Henchman* Deanesly was transferred to an RAF air sea rescue launch from 37 RAF ASR based at Lyme Regis. Two of the crew, Wireless Operator Biff Turner and Petty Officer Charles Steel, helped Christopher aboard. The launch docked at Lyme Regis and Christopher was transported to the local hospital where he was admitted suffering from slight wounds. A short period of leave followed.

On the evening he was shot down, Squadron Leader Peter Devitt and the squadron's Intelligence Officer visited him. He was always keen on sweets and carried some with him when flying. Squadron Leader Peter Devitt commented on Christopher at the hospital: 'I could imagine these sweets floating around him during his time in the water.'

Having heard his account of the combat he was credited with a 'damaged' for the Dornier Do 17, this aircraft in fact being that coded A5+EA of the Geschwader Stab Sturzkampfgeschwader 1. The pilot, Unteroffizier Lengenbrink, died in the aircraft. The other two crew members were taken prisoner, one being slightly wounded. The aircraft was on a reconnaissance mission to identify targets in the Portland area.

Christopher wrote a number of letters home to his mother explaining in detail his daily routine at Warmwell and during the Battle of Britain. The following account is taken from one such correspondence dated 11 August 1940:

Intercepted a Ju 88 a few days ago, unfortunately just as I was getting close he went into cloud. We had dived from 17,000ft to 8,000ft at about 550mph. I shot a couple at him but that's all. We were just off the Needles. Perhaps just as well as the engine packed up [and] I was looking to get down just on the coast with self and aircraft intact. On a field of stubble and roots, I finished rolling 15yds from the fence. Both magneto drives had packed up, possibly because I had been pushing hard, but there was no alternative. I thought at first I had been shot and was livid!

He wrote again on 28 August:

I quite innocently achieved a certain amount of certain popularity this morning after a very boring hour. 7-8 at 12,000ft I was told to land. As I was on top of the aerodrome I pulled the nose down and screamed down from 12,000ft at about 450mph.

Unfortunately for me there was the usual, and very much disliked, parade at the time. The row I made was apparently terrific and the parade scattered! I flattened out at 400ft and made a good landing not noticing anything untoward.

Later at breakfast the C.O complained that the station C.O had raised hell and wanted to know who it was. I explained that I lost height rather rapidly and there was really nothing to take exception to.

Then, on 9 September 1940, he noted the following:

I had a brief encounter with a Ju 88 recently which I intercepted near Bournemouth. I chased him from 17,000ft to 8,000ft and was just getting him into range when he reached cloud and I saw him no more. Pity, finished up south-west of the Needles.

On 21 August, at the controls of Spitfire P9432, Christopher intercepted a large formation of Ju 88s over Bristol. He attacked a lone Ju 88 from astern but, due to his fuel being low, was forced to return to the airfield. Apparently no damage was observed when he attacked the aircraft so was unable to place any claim on this engagement, which he described later in a letter:

24th August 1940

Had a nice little shoot up of a jerry on Saturday unfortunately he took 5000 rounds from two of us without turning a hair.

After a long chase when he gave himself away by a vapour trail, we caught him up at the Bristol Channel at 21,000ft he dived to sea

Above: RAF Warmwell's airfield roller with Jumbo at the control. (Author's Collection)

---

level at between 400mph and 500mph and we could only just hold him. Even so I was well within range when I let him have it. It was a Ju 88, a very fine and fast machine which generally seems to get away.

On 26 September, Christopher flew Spitfire K9982. Being one of the oldest aircraft on the squadron there was no armoured plating protecting the fuel tank. He believed he was given this aircraft by his flight commander because he had damaged a number of aircraft in his short time with the squadron.

On this date a total of nine aircraft took-off to intercept a large formation of Ju 88s, with escorting Me 109s, at 15,000ft over the Isle of Wight. Christopher was flying as Green 1, with Sergeant Bill Kearsey as his No.2.

Moving in to attack a Ju 88 when he was fired on from behind by a Me 109. K9982 was badly damaged and he was wounded in the upper leg. 'There was an explosion in my cockpit,' he recalled, 'and the engine lost power and caught fire.'

With little option, being forced to bale-out over the Channel, he soon found himself floating down towards the sea suspended under his parachute: 'I wondered if I would be able to free myself from the aircraft so I thought to invert the aircraft, open the roof and let gravity do the rest. I looked up and saw the Spit envelop[ed] in flames.'

A large man, his stature was the reason he had quickly acquired the nickname 'Jumbo'. It was also one of the reasons he had been worried about exiting his stricken aircraft, hence flipping it over.

Pilot Officer Dudley Williams witnessed the action and made sure Christopher landed safely in the water. He contacted control and they tasked an ASR launch to pick him up.

A Lysander flew out and soon spotted him about 12 miles off the Needles. A rescue launch was directed towards him and for a second time he was picked up and taken to shore. Badly wounded in the leg, he was again admitted to hospital. He later commented that it had been a very expensive afternoon that day.

Due to his injuries, he was removed from flying duties to became a fighter controller. When he had fully recovered, he became a flight commander on a night fighter unit, 256 Squadron flying Defiants. During his time with 256, he claimed a further four victories, three of these on one sortie. As a result, he was awarded the Distinguished Flying Cross on 30 May 1941.

Christopher went on to serve with many other squadrons in the UK and abroad. After commanding 298 Wing in the Middle East from January to August 1943, for example, he took over 114 Wing until March 1944 when he was posted back to the UK. He became CFI at 107 OTU, training pilots on Dakotas for paratrooper and glider-towing operations. Having taken command of 575 Squadron, equipped with Dakotas, in December 1944, he took part in the Rhine crossings in March 1945, towing a glider.

Leaving the RAF, with the rank of Wing Commander, in September 1945, he bought a small plastics factory in Birmingham that he successfully expanded to a business eventually employing about 150 people. He died in February 1998. Following his death, his daughter recalled that: 'He always said he enjoyed the war, which might sound strange, but he enjoyed the challenges he was given. He certainly did not think he was the best pilot or anything.'

Christopher 'Jumbo' Deanesly was one of the characters in the squadron and is well remembered for his humour and his size. His service with the RAF made him reflect on life, which was encapsulated in the words of a letter to his mother: 'It made me value how precious existence is.'

DEVITT, Squadron Leader Peter Kenneth
No.90080

Peter was born on Whit Sunday, 4 June 1911 at 05.30 hours. He grew up in Kent having the ambition to fly from a young age. He spent many happy years as a boy growing up watching the First World War from his garden due to having a large anti-aircraft battery in a nearby field. He had always said to his family that his first recollection of wanting to fly was in 1914 when he saw a silver balloon appear in the sky at a very low height. There was a sudden scattering of sand on his pram and he believed, after that moment, that he was destined to fly.

He was educated at Sherborne School, Dorset. In 1930 he learned to fly, at the age of 19, at West Malling. On 14 March 1932, he was commissioned in the RAF and continued his training at RAF Filton near Bristol. His dedication was noticed by many of his fellow flyers and his seniors. On 13 July 1933, he was given command of 600 Squadron Auxiliary Air Force, which was based at RAF Hendon, attaining the rank of pilot officer. He continued to run the squadron, reaching the rank of flight lieutenant on 24 August 1939.

On the outbreak of war, Peter was called-up for full-time service and posted as a fighter controller to the Operations Room at RAF Tangmere. His aim, however, was to fly. So, he came up with a plan to get himself in charge of a fighter squadron. His brother, Howson, who was also serving in the RAF as a commissioned officer, was extremely good at electronics, which would make him ideal for Peter's job. Together they put their case forward to Air Commodore John Hawtrey at Fighter Command explaining that Peter would like to take control of the next fighter squadron that became available and that Howson could take over Peter's position at Tangmere. This plan worked and on 1 February 1940, Peter received a signal to report to 152 Squadron at Acklington as the new commanding officer.

He soon discovered the main role of the squadron was to carry out escort patrols for shipping travelling up and down the East Coast. Peter was promoted to the rank of squadron leader on 1 June 1940.

Cuthbert Orde's sketch of Squadron Leader Peter Devitt. (Courtesy of the RAF Museum)

On 10 July, Air Vice-Marshal Richard Saul, Air Officer Commanding No.13 Group (which had responsibility for defending the north of Great Britain), called Peter into his office and explained:

> Devitt you are on your way tomorrow to Warmwell in Dorset. Small grass fields where there is an Armament training school. This will be removed soon so you will have the field to yourselves, and under 10 Group with Middle Wallop as your sector HQ. You are likely to be pretty busy as many convoys pass by Portland, the Naval Base there has quite a bit of aerial activity lately and this is why a Squadron has been asked for. My best wishes to you all. Good hunting and the best of luck.

On 11-12 July, the squadron duly said its farewells to RAF Acklington and set course on its 400-mile journey to Warmwell. The transport and stores travelled by road and took a further twenty-four hours to reach their destination.

Peter once reflected on the fact that the squadron was greeted at RAF Warmwell by cloud and loud rain, as well as having been placed on immediate notice to scramble. Indeed, during its first evening at its new home the squadron scrambled to engage enemy aircraft over Portland. These turned out to be a formation of Ju 87s. Peter remembers this engagement taught the squadron some very valuable lessons on the tactics of the Luftwaffe.

As squadron leader, there were many other aspects to Peter's job, such as signing for aircraft spares, writing letters to families of deceased pilots, messing functions and so on. On one occasion, when he was carrying out paperwork in his office, the air-raid warning siren sounded. He rushed down to dispersal but was too late to jump into an aircraft and get into the air. He sought cover into the nearest slit-trench from where he could do little but watch as enemy bombs fell around him. The experience was such that he later declared that: 'I would much rather have been in the air.'

Pilot Officer Dennis Fox-Male was one member of the squadron who remembered Devitt:

> Peter [was] aged about 31 years old, he was a member of the Auxiliary Air Force, with a lot of hours in his logbook. Being several years older than most of the pilots showed a shrewd steadiness which gave confidence to all the others. He had been at school at Sherbourne and it was ironic that he led 152 on that classic

interception towards the end of September when the enemy bombers jettisoned their load on Sherbourne [*sic*] School. He was probably the most unpopular 'Old Shirburnian'!

The incident referred to by Pilot Officer Dennis Fox-Male occurred on 30 September 1940, the squadron having been scrambled at 16.08 hours. Peter recounted his memories of the events that day to Sherborne School's historian, A.B. Gourlay, in 1950 (the following being quoted from the Old Shirburnian Society's website):

On this particular day, September 30th 1940, we had approximately 5 minutes in which time we were to take off and climb at our maximum rate of climb 1500 feet per minute to 20,000 feet. When airborne with 8 aircraft (all I could muster, and some of those should not have flown by peace time standards) I was ordered by Sector Control to proceed as quickly as possible to Yeovil, where a raid of 50 plus was approaching.

On arrival at approximately Yeovil (covered by cloud) there was no sign of the enemy. Thinking that perhaps they had delivered their bombs and swung round through 180 degrees to starboard, as they had done on a previous Bristol raid, I turned the Squadron eastwards in the hope of picking them up. They had obviously turned this way so as not to be silhouetted up against a background of white cloud for our fighters to pick up. It is always more difficult to pick up a camouflaged aircraft from above and with the earth below, but a fighter must have the advantage of height, in order to deliver his full weight in the first attack. A few seconds after I had spotted them, I saw their bombs falling away from beneath their bellies.

On looking down to see what the target was to my horror I saw the old school courts, which I knew so well. I was at that time just in position to attack, which I did, but was molested by a pack of Me 109s which I had not noticed sitting up above the Heinkels, and above me as well. I could not see much of where the bombs fell, as I was too intent on what was going on around me. I did, however, see in one instant a great deal of smoke around the old buildings, and so knew there must be some hits, and damage, and probably casualties. We eventually got through the German Fighters, and into the bombers, but with so few aircraft and so many to slaughter (we accounted for only 2 Heinkels and 1 Me 109), for no loss to our Pilots, but with many

Spitfire UM-A crash-landed on 25 September near Skew Bridge, Newton St Loe. (Courtesy of Andy Saunders)

bullet holes, all of which had to be patched before our next engagement which was that evening, when a small raid attacked Portland Bill.

Returning to earlier events, on 25 July, Peter was flying as Red 1, with Pilot Officer Richard Inness as his No2:

> S/Ldr Devitt attacked a Me 109, but he himself was attacked from the rear and tail of his a/c was hit by cannon. He turned sharply to the right and was unable to see whether or not the Me 109 went down out of control. Rounds fired: 210

Peter was credited with a 'damaged' for this engagement.

Another period that Peter recalled in his memoirs, *Reminiscences*, and that has caused some confusion, is a crash-landing he performed in text-book fashion. On 25 September 1940, he led the squadron in an engagement with a large formation of He 111s at a height of 23,000ft. The enemy aircraft were attacking targets in the Bristol area.

Peter received a direct hit from the raiders' return fire. At this point he then saw, to his horror, a row of high tension power cables directly in front him, as well as a railway line to his starboard side. As the enemy rounds had caused a fuel leak, and he was covered in fuel, he switched off the ignition to prevent the aircraft from catching fire. He then dropped to about 5,000ft at a speed of 400mph. The aircraft's self-sealing fuel tank did not seem to work as fuel was still leaking out.

Searching for a landing site, Peter spotted a field where he could perform a belly-landing. He then saw beyond that there was another a field which looked a safer site to land. He extended his glide, pushing his aircraft into a steep turn over a road, but while performing this he noticed more electricity cables stretched across his path. He was travelling at about 80mph, some 30ft from the ground and with a dead stick.

All Peter could do was pray and hope for the best. His aircraft settled and slid along for a short time with Peter's head hard against the windscreen of his cockpit. He had come down in a field near Skew Bridge, Newton St Loe, about 3 miles west of Bath.

On gathering himself together, a few moments later he realised, to his surprise, that there was a lady standing by his aircraft. As the Spitfire had landed on its belly she was almost at the same height as him and was patiently waiting while brandishing a cup of tea in her hand. The refreshment was, as Peter himself described, 'unforgettable'.

There was little respite for Peter and on 25 September he destroyed a He 111. Two more He 111s were damaged on 30 September. He also claimed a 'probable' Me 109 on 18 October: On this occasion he was flying with Pilot Officer Dudley Williams. They intercepted a large formation of enemy aircraft that was attacking shipping in a convoy near Portland Bill. They raced after the Germans and caught up with five Me 109s returning home towards the French coast. They were at 10,000ft. The rear Me 109 was weaving behind as 'tail end Charlie'. They attacked the formation of fighters from below, not the normal practice. Both Peter and Dudley fired a short burst and pulled away to port and starboard respectively. As they withdrew they only saw three Me 109s so believed that two enemy aircraft had been shot down – both pilots confirmed they saw bits coming off the enemy aircraft when firing on them.

On 30 October, Peter received a telephone call from Air Vice-Marshal Sir Quintin Brand, the Air Officer Commanding No.10 Group, which covered south-west England and South Wales. Brand explained that he felt Peter had done long enough as a squadron leader and should be promoted to wing commander. He was subsequently posted to the headquarters of No.9 Group at Preston.

Peter continued in the RAF, commanding many more squadrons during the war. He finished his career as a squadron leader in the Royal Auxiliary Air Force's 615 (County of Surrey) Squadron from 1949 to 1950. He died in 1997.

The stress that Peter was placed under during the Battle of Britain must have been immense. It has been said that he would have whiskey with his breakfast to help him through the day.

It was not uncommon for Peter to give his pilots a forty-eight-hour leave pass to help them relax from the pressures of battle. He is remembered fondly by Pilot Officer Roger Hall: 'He was about 27 at this time, married and with two children. Peter was fairly wealthy and had been a member of Lloyd's for some years. He was a debonair sort of person, an excellent pilot and a very capable leader.'

FOX-MALE, Pilot Officer Dennis
No.78660

Dennis was born on 28 June 1915, Oxshott, Surrey. He was educated at Wellington College and Trinity College, Oxford, where he studied Jurisprudence. He joined the University Air Squadron on 1 November

1934, learning to fly Avro Tutors and Hawker Harts, and remained a member until 26 July 1936.

After leaving Oxford he qualified and practised as a solicitor. On the outbreak of war, he was called-up for full-time service, being posted to 7 EFTS, Desford, on 12 April 1940. From there he moved to RAF Cranwell on 10 June, before being posted to 7 OTU, Harwarden, on 17 September to complete his initial training. He duly completed his conversion to Spitfires and was posted to 152 Squadron on 28 September 1940:

> I reached 152 Squadron with 175 hours solo and 85 hours dual flying, more than the average pilot but only 20% on monoplanes and the total included 15 hours on Spitfires. My first day at Warmwell was spent in drawing equipment, getting intelligence information and diving into air raid shelters. There I met a tall young WAAF Officer with the unusual Christian name of Kuni. She was engaged to and later married Jumbo Deanesley.

One of Dennis' closest friends at the squadron was Pilot Officer Norman Hancock:

> Dennis Fox-Male was a tall well-built young man of considerable charm. He was of course known in the Squadron as 'Foxy' and was very friendly and helpful towards me as a new member at the beginning of October. We did fly together on several occasions.
>
> Like most of us he was fond of his pint in the evenings and joined in Mess parties with enthusiasm. He was also adept at producing amended versions of the somewhat dubious songs we used to sing.
>
> On one occasion, he landed on the airfield having forgotten to put his wheels down and admitted regretfully afterwards that he was a better solicitor than a pilot.

In a speech he delivered at his local parish church some years later, Dennis once described in detail what it was like to be in aerial combat:

> You're in a small single-engine aeroplane. You have climbed to this great height in the company of eleven other pilots which has given you confidence. But you have been worried about your oxygen supply and whether you have adjusted it properly because you

39: Pilot Officer Dennis Fox-Male. (Courtesy of the Fox-Male family)

know that without oxygen you will die! And you have only used it once before.

Your cockpit hood is open for better visibility and the temperature is 20 degrees below freezing point. But you get some warmth from the engine in front of you, and anyway fear drives out any feeling of cold.

You screw up your eyes to look into the sun, and then you whip your head around to stare into the burning blue sky above because at 30,000ft the sky above is burning blue. And then if you have time you glance down at the patchwork quilt work below, the fields and woods the rivers and towns. And you know that only by the grace of God and with your limited skills can you return to your home aerodrome which if you can see it is larger than the smallest postage stamp. And then the bullets hit you, if you're lucky you die at once; if you are unlucky you are in a crippled plane from which you cannot escape, as you are severely wounded. And it is a long way, five miles down to earth and the great Re-awakening.

On 10 October I was on my third patrol as section leader, Green 1, flying to the port side of Boy Marrs who led the flight with Zag as my No2. He was at about 15,000 feet; the weather was fine with cumulus cloud in large bunches. Skirting around one of these in close formation I suddenly saw to my left a Me 109 coming towards me. It passed about 20 yards and the pilot and I looked at each other. We continued in formation but I did not know that Zag had pulled round in a right turn in an attempt to catch the 109, went into a spin and lost several thousand feet so I was quite unprotected.

The next thing I knew was my glycol tank started leaking. I immediately thought of Cocky's advice … 'If you get a bullet in the glycol tank, bail out before you catch fire.' I was green so I waffled about in the air and started to unplug my oxygen and my radio and opened the hood. All of the other aircraft had disappeared and I was just going through the drill to get out, when I noticed the glycol had stopped coming out. The engine seemed okay and I made my way back to Warmwell, landing last and rather sheepishly. I found out that apart from some bullets to the cockpit, one had gone clean over my head from behind and through the glycol tank about three inches from the top. The excess had flowed out but there was plenty left in the tank so the engine never overheated.

He was not credited with any confirmed 'kills' during the Battle of Britain, though he did fly numerous operational sorties during this period. On 10 October, when 'B' Flight was scrambled to intercept an X-raid, he was flying with Sergeant Josef Szlagowski as his No.2. They were patrolling at a steady altitude when they were 'bounced' by Me 109s. The flight commander, Pilot Officer Eric 'Boy' Marrs, screamed 'Break' on the R/T and the flight broke in all directions. It states in the squadron ORB that Dennis returned to Warmwell due to a glycol leak caused by a bullet hole.

Dennis also recalled an incident on 28 November:

> The squadron was released for lunch except for one section of two, Watson and myself. We were kept at dispersal for half an hour and joined the rest in the mess. Where most of them had finished their meal Doc and I were just tucking into tinned fruit salad – a luxury in those days – when a mess waiter came round and told us that the squadron had been called to readiness.
>
> We doubled back to dispersal with the others but nothing happened until nearly 4 o'clock when the squadron was scrambled and told to patrol the Isle of Wight at 2500 feet. Boitel-Gill led the squadron, Boy was 'B' Flight leader with Doc as his number 2. Dudley Williams was Green section leader and I was the weaver for 'B' Flight. A Pole, Sgt Klein, weaved behind 'A' Flight. We reached the Isle of Wight at about 2000 feet and from the radio conversion we knew that 609 squadron was in the air so it probably was a genuine raid. Weaving was always a difficult and tiring operation, nearly every time carried out by an inexperienced member of the squadron, as I still considered myself. I was concerned to cover the flight and keep up with it at the same time.
>
> An incoherent message came over the air which was later thought to have been from Sgt Klein who obviously turned towards the 109s and never came back. I was frantically weaving and saw nothing until I saw a 109 dive past and below Boy Marrs. His number 2, Doc [Watson], was gliding out of formation with some glycol streaming from his tank. Boy turned on his back and followed the 109 down. Soon we heard him say that he had shot the enemy plane down into the sea. The squadron regrouped and soon we were ordered to return to Warmwell and land.

Above: Pilot Officer Dennis Fox-Male can be seen top left next to Pilot Officer Ian Bayles in this picture taken outside dispersal. (Author's Collection)

Writing in a similar vein, he remembered flying on a morning patrol after a night out:

> I think we all three were feeling the effects of the night before and I know that I felt quite light-headed. I got into the air in close formation and ten minutes later as we climbed hard, we were told it was a false alarm and the enemy plane had turned back. Permission was asked to do some practice flying, the Flight Commander ordered us into close formation and dived for the Branscombe Towers Hotel. We felt that as our sleep had been interrupted we did not see why the civilians in their comfortable beds should not be fully aroused. We beat up the hotel at low level and then returned to Warmwell awake and invigorated to enjoy breakfast as the rest of the squadron were wiping the sleep from their eyes.

Dennis left the squadron on 9 July 1941. He was posted to 59 OTU at Crosby-on-Eden as an instructor. He went back to operational duties in 1942 and was posted to 242 Squadron at RAF Turnhouse. Promoted to flight lieutenant on 7 September 1942, Dennis remained with the squadron when it moved to North Africa in September 1942 and remained there until 5 March 1943.

Being released from the RAF in 1946 as a flight lieutenant. He resumed his legal career and was a partner in the family firm of London solicitors, Taylor and Humbert. In 1975 he retired with his wife Angela to live in the Channel Island of Alderney.

He died on 1 April 1986.

HALL, Pilot Officer Roger Montagu Dickenson No.43009

Roger was born on 12 August 1917. He was educated at Haileybury College from 1931 to 1935. He was accepted into the Royal Military Academy, Sandhurst, in 1936, and joined the Royal Tank Regiment in 1938. However, he suffered a period of poor mental health and did not return to his unit until the end of that year.

In 1939 Roger decided to join the RAF, as he explained: 'The reason I wanted to transfer to the RAF was the romance, the beauty of flight.' His transfer was accepted and in March 1940 he was posted to 7 EFTS, Desford, where he completed his initial training on Tiger Moths. In early August Roger went to No.1 School of Army Co-operation at Old Sarum, Wiltshire, to finish his training. He completed this three weeks later.

Now a trained fighter pilot, Roger was posted to 152 Squadron on 29 August: 'I arrived after midnight and the rain was pouring off the roofs of the wooden huts in continuous streams. It was blowing a gale from the sea as it often did in these parts and every now and again the downpour became caught up in the wind and driven horizontally.'

Roger was assigned to 'A' flight which was commanded by Flight Lieutenant Derek Boitel-Gill. On 2 September, he started his first operational day with the squadron on dawn readiness. He was soon in the air and engaged a lone Ju 88 that was returning to France across the Channel after a reconnaissance mission. 'Cocky' Cox hit the bomber, which exploded, and 'the intermingled mass of flaming wreckage fell into the sea'.

On another occasion Roger was part of a flight that scrambled to intercept an X-raid. The weather was bad and Roger heard the order to 'Pancake' and headed for home. As he neared the aerodrome, he noticed that his engine was not running correctly, though as he believed he could make it home he did not initially pay much attention to the problem. But, over the Wiltshire countryside his engine finally gave up:

> I was below cloud base at a height of 1,500ft. In these circumstances, I had no other choice but to make a force-landing. I decided to put the machine down on the main road running between Salisbury and Andover. I put my wheels down and manoeuvred into a favourable approach position. I came straight in line of the road which seemed to be clear of traffic but at the last moment two lorries drove in sight. I was compelled to divert to a small field. I side-slipped my aircraft violently and my port wing struck the ground. It buckled and tore itself away throwing the remainder of the plane on its starboard wing, which in turn came off together with the landing wheels. The fuselage slithered along the ground for about fifty yards until it stopped. The aircraft was a complete write-off but the only injury I suffered was a grazed knee.

Pilot Officer Dennis Fox-Male remembers with humour that:

> P/O R.M.D. ('Sammy') Hall was in 'A' Flight … he always seemed fairly mad, in the nicest sort of way, and nothing like as intense as he now appears to have been. When returning from a patrol he would weave violently in the circuit of the airfield and we would say 'there's Sammy again flying his Spit like a bloody tank'.

Roger claimed two enemy aircraft as 'damaged' during the Battle of Britain – a Bf 110 on 27 September, off the coast of Swanage, and a He 111 over Exmoor on 7 October. Like many of the other pilots that flew during this period, Roger's view on life changed and he increasingly turned to religion to help him survive.

He left the squadron in December, being posted to the newly-formed 255 Squadron, a night fighter unit based at RAF Kirton-on-Lindsey. He claimed the squadron's first victory, a He 111. Roger also served with 72 and 91 squadrons as a flight commander and was awarded the Distinguished Flying Cross on 24 November 1942.

Pilot Officer Roger Hall. (Author's Collection)

Above: Pilot Officer Roger Hall standing by a 152 Squadron Spitfire. P/O Pooch is standing on the wing. (Author's Collection)

Below: A group of 152 Squadron personnel. They are, left to right, Roger Hall, Richard Innes, Graham Cox, P/O Pooch, Ferdie Holmes and Ian Bayles. (Author's Collection)

Roger lost his flying category in 1942 due to another bout of mental illness and was transferred to the Administration Branch of the RAF. He left the RAF in 1944 and joined the RAFVR, finishing his service in 1960 as a flying officer. He wrote a memoir, *Clouds of Fear*, which was first published in 1975: An abridged version was later released as *Spitfire Pilot*.

He was living in Dover when he died in December 2002.

HANCOCK, Pilot Officer Norman Edward
No.83266

Norman was born on 12 May 1920. He was educated at Lewes Grammar School, East Sussex. He did not have any specific civilian job before joining the RAF.

Norman joined the RAFVR in July 1939 as an airman u/t pilot. He was called-up for full-time service on 1 September 1939, being posted to ITW Trinity Hall, Cambridge, on 5 September. On 26 March 1940, he moved to 12 EFTS, Prestwick, and then to 5 FTS, Sealand, on 26 May.

With Norman's training complete he was commissioned on 10 August and was posted to 7 OTU, to convert to Spitfires, the following day. On completion, he moved to 65 Squadron, which was based at RAF Hornchurch, on 3 September. After a short period there, he moved to 152 Squadron on 1 October.

His life with the squadron was like any other pilot during this period: 'Dawn readiness on frosty mornings at our dispersal hut followed by welcome bacon and egg breakfast in the Officers Mess. Long periods during the day of waiting for the telephone to ring at the same hut.' He remembers well when the telephone would ring and the order to 'scramble' rang out:

> When the telephone rang it usually meant an order to patrol at say Angels 15 or 15,000ft over Weymouth or the Isle of Wight, as a section of two, a flight or even a squadron. The target was usually Me 109s with which we mixed and shot at or were ourselves shot at.

Norman later commented on the part he played during the Battle of Britain: 'As regards to our thoughts we just reckoned we were doing the job we were trained for.'

Pilot Officer Norman Hancock. (Courtesy of the Hancock family)

On 28 November, Norman claimed a 'probable' on a Bf 110, though further investigation revealed that this was a confirmed 'kill'. Norman clearly remembers the action:

> I got separated from the squadron after a mix-up but still had enough fuel left to stay up in the air. I decided to do what fighter pilots should do and climb up into the sun and look around. I saw this aircraft 3,000ft below me and dived on it.
>
> I attacked the 110 from behind and set its port engine on fire. It immediately went into a very steep dive and even at full throttle I could not stay with it. I gave it a final burst and turned for home as we were half way across the Channel and my fuel was getting low. Later information stated the crew of the 110 did not return hence it must have gone into the sea.

The aircraft involved, a Me 110 of 3 Auf Gruppe 31, coded 5D+SL, and with the *werk nummer* 2201, was returning to France. The crew of Leutnant Walter Burmeister (pilot) and Oberleutnant Alex Von Brixen (Bordfunker) were reported missing.

Norman was promoted to flying officer on 10 August 1941 and posted to 56 OTU, Sutton Bridge, on 22 October 1941, to carry out instructional duties. He was then posted to 128 Squadron as a flight commander, being awarded the Distinguished Flying Cross on 23 June 1944.

He left the RAF in March 1946, having attained the rank of squadron leader. Norman commented that, 'it's a matter of luck in war'.

HOGG, Flight Lieutenant Edward Sydney
No.70312

Edward was born on 10 January 1916 in Leeds, Yorkshire. He was educated at Leeds Grammar School and after his education worked in the family clothing business W.A. Hogg & Co.

Sydney, as he was more commonly known, joined the Reserve of Air Force Officers on a short service commission in March 1937 and was commissioned on 9 May that year. He carried out his intermediate and advanced training at 8 FTS Montrose.

On 19 January 1938, Sydney was posted to 66 Squadron at RAF Duxford, remaining there until he was posted to 11 FTS Perth, then onto

Pilot Officer Sydney Hogg. (Courtesy of the Hogg family)

Above: Flight Lieutenant Elise Withall (on the left) and Pilot Officer Sydney Hogg (centre) pictured with Sergeant Walker. (Author's Collection)

12 FTS Grantham as an instructor. Sydney remained at Grantham until 20 November 1939 when he was posted to 609 (West Riding) Squadron at Drem. He joined 152 Squadron at the beginning of 1940 when it was at Acklington.

It could often be said that while Sydney was at readiness at dispersal he would sit and relax under his Spitfire's wing, enjoying the sunshine and wait for the cry of 'scramble!'

On 8 August, flying as Green 1, he took-off with eight other squadron aircraft to patrol over Convoy *Peewit* as it passed Portland:

> Blue and Green sections on reaching 12,000ft over the convoy were attacked by 20 plus Me 109 from above, E/A dived out of the sun and a dog fight ensured immediately.
>
> Green section was attacked out of the sun by 4 Me 109s, Green 1 climbed steeply away. He found many Me 109s in pairs several thousand feet above, and attacked a Me 109 on the turn getting a

short burst into the tail. He then broke away when he found tracer going past him. He then attacked another Me 109 after which he saw black smoke coming from its engine but broke away when attacked by 3 Me 109s. He then saw Hurricane a/c attack a Me 109 and saw one Me 109 in difficulties and another go down in flames. He then made two further attacks on Me 109 which were ineffective as he himself was attacked. When about to attack another Me 109 and turning slightly at 400yds a second Me 109 passed him and shot down the first Me 109.

Sydney was extremely good with cars and mechanics, and found a way to use aviation fuel in his own car. The following is a story he told to one of his daughters some years later:

> He would regularly walk past the CO's office carrying two buckets of water to wash his car. In fact, the buckets contained aviation fuel which, somehow, he managed to run his car on. The CO apparently remarked on how clean Hogg kept his car.
>
> He was always good with engines and knew exactly what was wrong with his Spit when there was a problem.

On 12 August, again flying as Green 1, he engaged a large enemy force over St Catherine's Point on the Isle of Wight. Sydney's No.2 was Pilot Officer Walter Beaumont, who joined Sydney in attacking a Ju 88, which they both damaged. They then followed Blue Section and carried out a combined attack on another Ju 88, which Sydney last saw emitting black smoke after pieces had fallen off it. It force-landed on the Isle of Wight. Sydney was also given a 'damaged', and a 'shared' on another Ju 88.

Much physical and mental stress was placed on pilots in the Battle of Britain, and in mid-August, while over the Isle of Wight, he fell asleep in mid-air during a combat. He woke to find an enemy aircraft in his gun sight and his thumb on the gun button. When he landed, he asked if anybody saw this action – which they had not.

There were two pilots with the surname of Hogg on the squadron, the other being Pilot Officer Richard Hogg. As Sydney was considerably thinner and smaller than his fellow pilot he was nicknamed 'Finhogg'.

On 23 August, flying as Blue 1, he and his No.2 intercepted a lone Ju 88:

Above: A group of 152 Squadron's pilots, comprising, left to right, Richard Inness, Sydney Hogg, Walter Beaumont and Charles Warren. (Author's Collection)

2 A/C Blue section took off from Warmwell 1553-1620, 3 miles S.W of Lulworth Cove at 4,000ft intercepted Ju 88 when Blue 1 and 2 attacked E/A went into cloud followed by Blue 1 who attacked from quarter when return fire ceased.

Blue 1 then attacked from astern. Blue 2 then attacked and saw black smoke coming from fuselage of E/A which crashed into the sea 25 miles south of Bournemouth.

> Both A/C landed at Warmwell. 1 A/C temporarily US with bullet hole in leading edge of port wing.

Sydney was posted to 58 OTU, Grangemouth, in October 1940, as an instructor. Carrying out more advance instructional courses at CFS Upavon, he was posted to 4 FTS in 1941.

In 1943 he was posted to Canada and served at a training school at Moose Jaw, Saskatchewan, returning to the UK in June 1943. He retired from the RAF as a wing commander in October 1945. He died on 23 December 1986.

HOGG, Pilot Officer Richard Malzard
No.33486

Richard was born on 2 July 1919 in the parish of St Peter on the Channel Island of Jersey. He was one of two brothers. His father had been a Royal Navy Commander in the First World War. He was educated at Victoria College.

He enlisted as an officer cadet at RAF Cranwell on 28 April 1938. Due to the outbreak of war his course was cut short and he passed-out in September 1939. He was awarded the R.M. Groves Memorial flying prize as the best all round pilot of his intake. He was commissioned on 23 October of that year.

Richard was posted to 11 Group Pool at RAF St Athan on 24 October where he was instructed in flying Blenheims. On completion, he was posted to 145 Squadron at Croydon.

He had a flying accident on 10 February 1940, while flying Blenheim K7114. He collided with another aircraft but, luckily, both returned safely to the airfield.

In July, he was posted to 152 Squadron just before their move south to Warmwell. Being placed into 'A' Flight he soon settled in with the squadron carrying out the normal routine of escort duties and practising formation flying. As mentioned previously, because there were two Hoggs in the squadron, Richard, the larger of the two, became known as 'Fathogg'.

On 25 July, flying as Yellow 2 and in company with Flying Officer 'Jumbo' Deanesly, Richard became involved in a combat over Portland with a large formation of enemy aircraft:

RICHARD MALZARD HOGG

P/O Hogg, Yellow 2, followed F/O Deanesly, Yellow 1, in a No1 attack from dead astern and fired one burst of approx. eight seconds from 250yds closing to 75yds. He experienced cannon fire from the

Above: Pilot Officer Richard Hogg. (Author's Collection)

rear gunner and concluded that this came from one gun. Rounds fired: 2,225

Richard was credited with a 'damaged' for the attack on the Do 17 and a shared 'kill', with Sergeant Ralph Wolton, of a Ju 87. Richard's next engagement was on 12 August: 'Yellow 1 and Yellow 2 [Hogg] attacked a Ju 88 which landed on sea 20 miles S.E of Sandown. Rounds fired: 2,800.'

On 21 August, Richard was flying as part of Red Section when the three aircraft took off to patrol east of Swanage. A lone Ju 88 was seen around the area of the Needles at an altitude of 4,000ft. Red Section was vectored to engage the raider, which they did in a No.1 line astern attack: 'White trails of smoke were seen coming from the E/A mainly from the Port engine. The E/A then came down to sea level. Approximately one and half of a minute it crashed into the sea.' Red Section returned safely back to the airfield with no losses.

At 17.30 hours on 25 August Richard, having already flown a number of sorties that day, took-off as part of a squadron scramble to intercept an enemy formation over Portland. Flight Lieutenant Derek Boitel-Gill was leading the squadron with headings from Control keeping the pilots updated on the enemy formation's size and direction of travel. The Spitfires, however, were soon 'bounced' by Me 109s.

Two of the Spitfires, Richard's and that of Pilot Officer Timothy Wildblood, were hit by the fire from the Me 109s. Richard was killed instantly. Sergeant Denis Robinson was one of the last people to see Richard alive and witnessed his death: 'My gut feeling is that Richard may not even have seen his attacker. He was a good aggressive fighter pilot but sadly had so little time to develop his skills.'

Richard's aircraft, R6810, crashed into the sea. His body was never recovered and he is remembered on the Runnymede Memorial. Squadron Leader Peter Devitt remembered the fate of the two pilots:

> We lost two experienced pilots that day. I was very sorry to lose them; they were both charming young men.
>
> There had been a number of raids in the Dorset area that day by the Luftwaffe; the Me 109s were from Jagdgeschwader 53 and had been escorting Ju 88s from Kampfgeschawader 51. Their mission was to bomb RAF Warmwell … The Me 109s had broken away from the bomber formation early to look for RAF fighters.

Squadron Leader Devitt went on to detail the events that followed:

> Flight Lieutenant 'Jumbo' Deanesly had been put in charge of the 'Committee of Adjustment'. This [meant] being in charge of, and responsible for, the correct disposal of Richard's personal belongings.
>
> Dick Hogg owned a 10hp Standard car. This was apparently collected by a Naval officer who I took to be Dick's brother. However, Ted Hogg's service was also in the RAF. He was a good aggressive fighter pilot; I admired him. The person who came to

collect the car was [in fact] Richard's father, Mr Philip Hogg, who was serving in the Royal Navy at the time.

Both brothers would be killed in action during the Second World War while serving in the RAF. Richard's other brother, Edward, was killed in 1941 while at the controls of a Spitfire involved in a flying accident.

Hogg's father also served in the Royal Navy in the Second World War. According to Deanesly, he was in naval uniform when he picked up Richard's belongings after his death.

Below: A Jersey Post stamp depicting Richard Hogg's aircraft. (Author's Collection)

HOLLAND, Sergeant Kenneth Christopher
No.754503

Kenneth was born on 29 January 1920 in Sydney, New South Wales. His father served in the Australian Imperial Force in the First World War. In 1916, while based in the UK, he met Kenneth's mother, who was from Cork, Ireland.

Sergeant Ken Holland. (Author's Collection)

Kenneth was educated at the following schools: Wellington Street, North Bondi Public School, Campbell Parade and Randwick Intermediate High. He grew up having witnessed historic moments such as the building of the Sydney Harbour Bridge, as well as experiencing the poverty which that Australia in the early 1930s.

Having arrived in the UK in the mid-1930s, he lived in Camelford, Cornwall, in the care of a guardian, Mr Hugh Ripley.

Kenneth attended college in 1936 and 1937, where he trained to become an aeronautical engineer. He went on to work for Airspeed Ltd. Predictably, he soon acquired the nickname 'Dutchy'. One of his friends at the college was Philip Markham, who remembers Kenneth well:

> I remember Dutchy very clearly. He was a cheerful, outgoing person but not so extroverted as most Australians I met later! He could be quiet and private at times, had strong opinions, could be stubborn and occasionally exhibited flashes of temper. We worked and played together, and he was a really good friend. Jo, my fiancée, and I were very fond of him. He left us fifty pounds in his will to assist us in getting married. Although he knew it was planned for November, less than two months after he died.

Another of his friends at college was John Lindsay:

> His guardian used to come to Portsmouth during term time and we would be taken out to lunch at the Royal Beach Hotel, which to us lads was a great treat. In 1938 Dutchy bought himself a new Imperial 250cc motorcycle on which we had many a jaunt.

Kenneth joined the RAFVR in 1939 as a u/t pilot, being called-up at the outbreak of war. After completing his initial flying training, he went to 11 ETS, Scone near Perth, Scotland. He joined 152 Squadron at Warmwell in August 1940. He arrived there late at night and on reporting to the orderly office found that there was 'nothing doing'. He met a friend in Weymouth and stayed there overnight. It seems as if the 'nothing doing' extended to the 18th as, after breakfast at his hotel, he went off for a swim, then lunch and tea out.

Ken returned to Warmwell on 19 August, where he was introduced to Squadron Leader Peter Devitt. He was initially allocated to 'A' Flight but later that day moved to 'B' Flight. Throughout the rest of the month Ken was involved in most of the squadron's operations.

On 15 September, flying as Green 3, he took off as part of 'B' Flight. Climbing to 15,000ft, a large formation of He 111s was spotted seven miles south-west of Portland. There was no fighter escort. When the enemy spotted the Spitfires they turned north-east, only for 'B' Flight to pass them whilst coming in too fast from the opposite direction. The He 111s dropped their bomb load on Portland Harbour and turned for home.

Above: Major Heinz Cramer.
(Deutsche Bundesarchiv)

Green Section then spotted a lone bomber at the rear of the formation and went in for the attack. The following is taken from the squadron combat report:

> Green section 3 a/c carried out an attack on a straggler from enemy formation. Green 1 made astern attack concentrating fire on starboard engine broke away left and downwards. Green 3 then attacked with 5 second burst from astern and above and black smoke poured from starboard engine and it began to lose height.

On 17 September, Ken was involved in the destruction of a Ju 88A-1, *werk nummer* 3188 and coded L1+XC. The other pilots with him in Blue Section were Pilot Officer Eric Marrs and Flying Officer O'Brian. Piloted by Leutnant Otto Heinrich, of Lehrgeschwader 1, the Ju 88 crashed at Ladywell Barn at Imber on Salisbury Plain, Wiltshire, at 14.00 hours. On board was Major Heinz Cramer, the Gruppen Kommandeur of II/LG1.

For his part, Ken had to make an emergency landing at RAF Yatesbury because his engine was running very hot. After a check of the engine it was shown that it had been hit by enemy fire in three places.

Above: The wreckage of Cramer's Junkers Ju 88 being recovered by an RAF salvage team. (Courtesy of Frank Hayward)

Below: Having been 'shot up', Pilot Officer Ken Holland's Spitfire is pictured here after a force-landing at RAF Yatesbury. (Author's Collection)

The glycol and oil systems had been damaged and the starboard tyre was punctured.

A local resident, Frank Hayward, witnessed this aerial combat and subsequently provided this account:

> In 1940 I was 14 and lived in Holbrook Lane, Trowbridge, in Wiltshire with my family. Like all boys at the time I was a keen aircraft spotter, and often cycled off to visit RAF stations with my school friends, even as far as RAF Hullavington to watch aircraft taking off and landing …
>
> On 17th September I was at school in the morning but as normal I cycled home for lunch. Just as I was about to return to school I was alerted by the sound of aircraft and looking up I saw a Spitfire chasing a lone Ju 88, at around 5,000 feet. I remember seeing that the Spitfire was firing at the Ju 88 and the noise it made surprised me in the sense that it was a single 'burrrr' noise and not a 'rata tat tat' that I had expected.
>
> I'm certain that it was only one Spitfire I saw and not a formation of them. After the Spitfire fired on the Ju 88 a few times, the Spitfire suddenly broke off the attack and peeled away, much to my annoyance as I was getting very excited at the time and shouting at the Spitfire 'shoot it down, shoot it down!'
>
> Naturally I couldn't wait to tell my friends what I had seen. By this time the Ju 88 was heading in a south-east direction, towards Westbury White Horse, trailing smoke and was getting lower and lower. I don't think any of us knew at the time whether it crashed or not but the memory of that brief combat in the Battle of Britain has stayed with me ever since, and despite serving as a pilot for much of my 42 years in the RAF, this was the only time I saw one aircraft attack another for real.

Of interest is the fact that Major Heinz Cramer has stated the Ju 88 was on a solo sortie to bomb an aircraft factory at Speke, Liverpool. The Ju 88's observer, Leutnant Otto Heinrich, aged 21, was killed, while Cramer (29), the wireless operator, Oberfeldwebel Paul Stützel (27), and the air gunner, Feldwebel Fritz Schultz (25), were captured, the latter two with slight wounds. Major Heinz Cramer was awarded the Knight's Cross of the Iron Cross, in his absence, the day after he was shot down, for his services as Gruppen Kommandeur of II/LG1. He was a keen sportsman and had represented Germany at the Berlin Olympics in 1936.

After his capture and interrogation, he was sent to Camp 13 at The Hayes, Swanwick in Derbyshire, where there was a conference centre that had been converted in to a PoW camp. It was there that he met up with fellow Luftwaffe prisoners, including Oberleutnant Franz von Werra (of II/JG53), who later became famous as 'the one that got away' when he escaped from a train in Canada and returned to Germany via the USA, Mexico, South America and Spain and Italy.

While Franz von Werra was at Camp 13, he formed a small escape group to tunnel out of the camp, of which Major Heinz Cramer became the chairman. On the night of 17 December 1940, after nearly a month of tunnelling, Franz von Werra and Heinz Cramer broke out of Camp 13, together with Leutnant Walter Manhard (of 6/ZG 76), Leutnant Ernst Wagner (of 5/JG 54) and Oberleutnant Johannes Wilhelm (of StG 77). While Oberleutnant Franz von Werra managed to bluff his way on

to Hucknall aerodrome and attempted to steal a brand new Hawker Hurricane before being apprehended, the others, including Heinz Cramer, were soon rounded up.

After the escape attempt Heinz Cramer remained as a PoW until 1947. He later joined the reformed Bundeswehr in 1956 and retired in 1966 as a brigadier general.

A further twist that resulted from the shooting down of L1+XC came in the form of the court martial of one Lieutenant Colonel (Acting Brigadier) Guy Percy Lumsden Drake-Brockman DSO MC, Royal Tank Regiment. On 17 September, Drake-Brockman had been the Officer Commanding the 21st Army Tank Brigade, elements of which had been training on Salisbury Plain near the crash site.

Above: Lieutenant Colonel Drake-Brockman. (Courtesy of the *Sunday Telegraph*)

Following their capture, two members of the Ju 88's crew were brought before Drake-Brockman, at which point he struck them. Drake-Brockman himself later explained: 'They spat on the floor, spat on my shoes, then spat on me and called me a bloody English swine. I don't know who could stand this spitting and insulting, this arrogance and beastliness, but I could not.'

An article in the *Daily Telegraph* of 18 September 1991, drawing on recently declassified files relating to the court martial, paints a somewhat different and more graphic version of events:

> The brigadier arrived 'clearly very enraged'. Major R.M. Millar, prosecuting, told the secret tribunal, 'He ordered the prisoners to take off their overalls; asked for a pocket knife and slit their trousers down the back and pulled off their belts so the trousers fell down around their ankles. He then drove his walking stick into the Luftwaffe major's [Cramer] groin, saying "You buggers, you have killed my mother". The German tried to protect his face and cried out. The brigadier then left the major and went to the other prisoner, who also put up his hands when he was struck in the groin.'
>
> The incident was watched by a crowd of booing soldiers, ATS girls and civilian workers, none of whom attempted to intervene.
>
> In a later incident, the brigadier told the German, 'If Adolf Hitler comes here we will tear his balls out one by one and you are lucky not to have yours torn out.' The German shrank back muttering, 'No, oh no'.

At his trial, Drake-Brockman was found guilty of 'behaviour prejudicial to good order and discipline of His Majesty's forces'. He was dismissed from the British Army on 14 November 1940. The *Milwaukee Sentinel* of 21 February 1942 provides information on Drake-Brockman's subsequent movements:

> Drake-Brockman, brigadier who was court-martialled out of the British Army for striking two German prisoners, has risen from ordinary tank trooper to major in the Canadian army in little more than a month.
>
> Anxious to get into the fight again under the colors of the empire, Drake-Brockman enlisted as a Canadian trooper Jan. 9, scrubbing floors, carrying coal and standing sentry duty.

His promotion in a single step to the rank of major, which has just come through, left him 'dumbfounded' with pleasant surprise. 'Great Country, this Canada,' he declared enthusiastically.

On the afternoon of 18 September, Ken and Pilot Officer Eric Marrs piled into Pilot Officer Peter O'Brian's car and headed off to locate the spot where L1+XC had crashed, their intention being to obtain a souvenir or two. Having set off at 15.00 hours, the journey took two hours. On their arrival the 152 Squadron pilots discovered, much to their dismay, that they were too late: It transpired that others, believed to be personnel from the Royal Tank Corps, had 'pinched things – almost everything from it'.

There was a crowd surrounding the machine, which had been roped-off in an attempt to keep sightseers and souvenir-hunters at bay. Ken and his colleagues, however, were allowed to climb all over what remained of the Ju 88. Despite the best efforts of the Army personnel, Ken and his friends claimed an 'altimeter and petrol tank dip stick – good condition' and an 'armoured pilot seat'. As Ken examined the Ju 88 he noticed where the Spitfires' bullets had struck, including in the radiator and the back of the pilot's back armour-plated seat.

On 19 September, Ken was flying as Green 2, with Pilot Officer Dudley Williams as Green 1, when he took-off from Warmwell to intercept a lone Ju 88 flying over the Channel. They spotted the aircraft at 10,000ft. However, due to a fault with his radio, Williams had to return to Warmwell leaving Ken to engage the raider alone. The following is taken from the squadron combat report for this engagement:

Green 2 saw the Ju 88 ahead and starboard quarter 2 miles away. Interception was due almost entirely to excellent instructions given by the controller. Green 2 gave chase and made alternative quarter attacks from left and right from 300-200 yards aiming first at the gunner's position then at each engine. E/A took only slight evasive action but mainly concentrated on heading for cloud to the south. Return fire ceased after first burst and black puff of smoke appeared after second. Green 2 continued attack on E/a now at 8,000ft dived vertically into the sea, both engines on fire. Ammunition being finished and engine missing Green 2 landed at Portsmouth aerodrome and having checked engine found it in order he returned to Warmwell. The E/A had what appeared to be a free cannon firing port side of the cockpit. This fire ceased after first burst. Fire from cannon was slow and regular while it lasted. Green 2 states that information on cannon fire should be treated with reserve. E/A had usual markings. Cloud was variable in height and thick 6/10ths cumulus, base 5,000ft.

Top varying from 11/14,000ft. R/T of Green 2 was indifferent but vectoring was excellent. No cine gun was carried. Rounds fired: 2,800 rounds, ranges above.

Ken also described the action:

As my ammunition was finished I flew on a northerly course, and came to the Isle of Wight.

My engine was missing slightly so I made for Portsmouth aerodrome, and before I finished checking the engine, I met up with some of 'the old gang' at the Airspeed works. When my Spitfire was declared all sound I ran up the engine, cleared out and shot up the works' in a final farewell.

On 25 September, Flying as Blue 2, Ken engaged a He 111 over Bath. He attacked several times before the bomber began to emit black smoke. Adopting a more cautious approach, he moved in to confirm the certainty of his 'kill', at the same time noticing a parachute open. But one of the bomber's crew was still manning a machine-gun and fired a short burst at Ken's Spitfire. One round hit the front of the Spitfire's cockpit, passed through the Perspex and hit Ken's head. It is believed that he was killed instantly.

Shortly afterwards, Flight Lieutenant Hudson investigated and reported:

Sergeant Holland came up at great speed, circled once to identify his quarry and opened fire at approx 400 yards from the rear and slightly to the port side. His first burst apparently took effect for the [Heinkel] He 111 rapidly began to lose height and circled as if looking for a landing. Sergeant Holland turned quickly and got in a second burst, turned again and at 2000 feet came up on the enemy's tail. This was his only mistake and was fatal as the rear gunner had not been silenced and was able to get in one burst at short range. This burst was fatal and the machine of Sergeant Holland dropped his nose and crashed.[2]

Above: Hauptmann Helmet Brandt's Ju 88 crash-landed at Woolverton. (Courtesy of Andy Saunders)

Both aircraft crashed close to each other in the fields of Church Farm at Woolverton, twelve miles south-east of Bath. A local resident witnessed the final moments of the RAF aircraft:

> The Spitfire broke its back as it crashed. I sent the gardener out to see if the pilot was all right – nothing could be done for him – he had been shot right through the head.

The Heinkel involved was from 6 Staffel, Kampfgeschwader 55. It had the code letters G1+EP and werk nummer 1525. The crew comprised Hauptmann Helmet Brandt (Staffelkapitän), Unteroffizier Hans-Fritz Mertz, Gefreiter Rudolf Beck, Oberfeldwebel Gunter Wittkamp, and Oberfeldwebel Rudolf Kirchhoff. Only the pilot, Brandt, survived when he baled out of his stricken aircraft.

Mrs Leslie Matthews was the wife of the farmer that owned Church Farm:

> Four of the five men in the crew managed to jump from their burning bomber, but they were too low and three killed. A fifth man failed to get out and his body was burnt beyond recognition in the wreckage.

This is believed to be Hauptmann Helmet Brandt at a London railway station, en route to the 'London Cage'. He ended in PoW camps in Canada. (Courtesy of Andy Saunders)

Tom Meadway was a local resident in 1940:

> I checked on the safety of my family and then went to the crash site near the war memorial, beside the Bath-Frome road, where the German bomber was burning fiercely.
>
> As I ran across the field I came across a German airman lying on the ground. He was alive and conscious, but badly wounded in several places by machine-gun bullets. I disarmed the airman, asking him if he spoke English. The German replied that he understood a little and told me in halting English how to remove the magazine from his loaded pistol.
>
> Another man arrived on the scene and between us we made the wounded airman comfortable, using his parachute as a pillow.

Though he had survived, Brandt was badly wounded, having received two bullet wounds to his right leg, as well as injuries to his right hand and his neck. Meadway continued his account:

> I lit a cigarette and placed it between the German's lips, an act that caused some of the women now present to become quite hostile. The German then told me his name was Brandt and that he was the pilot of the aircraft. I questioned him further and he revealed it was his first time in England and that he had a wife and a daughter in Munich.

Brandt noticed another crew member who was lying 30 yards from him and asked Tom to check the badges of rank to confirm the crewman's identity:

> By now a small crowd had gathered and I was kneeling by Brandt who became worried by some of the remarks being made. These comments, mainly by the women present, were to the effect that he had been killing women and children. To this Brandt replied he was only doing his duty, as our airmen were doing their duty over Germany. At that point I rebuked the crowd for their behaviour towards an enemy who was longer a danger to us.
>
> There was nothing of the so-called 'arrogant Nazi' about him. He was dignified and although nervous, as one would expect from anyone in his position, he gave an impression of great courage,

Pilot Officer Ken Holland's memorial stone near the A36 at **Woolverton.** (Author's Collection)

despite being surrounded by a hostile crowd while in a badly wounded condition and in an obvious state of shock.

One other incident remains clearly in my mind – a member of the Home Guard arrived, in civilian clothes but carrying a rifle, and took up a position at Brandt's feet. The German officer turned to me and said, 'Is he going to shoot me?' To which I replied that we didn't do that to prisoners-of-war in England and that he was safer now that when he had been in the air.

The final episode of the drama is one that still makes me feel ashamed. An ambulance finally arrived and Brandt was literally bundled in and driven off across the field at a speed which caused the rear wheels to leave the ground and must have caused the wounded man great distress. It was obviously done quite deliberately.

Ken's body was taken back to Warmwell and he was cremated at Weymouth Crematorium. The service was held on 2 October and his remains were removed by his guardian, Hugh Ripley, who subsequently erected a memorial at the crash site. The memorial was maintained by the wife of the farmer who owned the field at the time, Mrs Gladys Matthews, who also witnessed the crash.

In 1976, the memorial stone was moved to the side of the road as it was hindering farming in the field and was forgotten about, until in 1985, using funds raised by the local RAFA, the memorial was restored and placed in the local churchyard at Woolverton, where it resides today. Mr Ripley kept the urn containing Kenneth's ashes by the front window of his house until his own death.

Kenneth Christopher Holland was only 20 years old at the time of his death. He was the youngest Australian to die in the Battle of Britain.

HOLMES, Flying Officer Frederick Henry
No.76583

Frederick was born on 24 November 1913 in Nottingham. He was educated at People's College, Nottingham. He was a keen musician, winning awards for playing the piano. He was also a keen sportsman.

When he left school, he went to work in a bank and quickly rose to the position of manager. 'Freddie', or 'Ferdie' as he was more often known, joined the RAFVR in July 1938 as airman u/t pilot 741791, being called-up to full-time service in September 1939.

Above: Flying Officer Ferdie Holmes. (Courtesy of the Holmes family)

Ferdie carried out his training at 9 FTS and No.3 Bomb and Gunnery School before being posted to 152 Squadron on 18 June 1940. He moved south with the squadron and was soon in combat with the Luftwaffe.

On 25 July, flying as White 2, he was on patrol with nine other squadron aircraft when, at 11.15, hours a large formation of Ju 87s, Me 109s and one Do 17 was spotted at 11,000ft flying 20 miles south of Portland in a north-west direction. The squadron broke into pairs to attack the enemy formation:

Ferdie relaxing with his daughter. (Courtesy of the Holmes family)

Sgt. Wolton White 1, and P/O Holmes, White 2, also fired at the
Do17 which came down in flames in the vicinity of Fleet. Rounds
fired: 240

On 18 August the squadron intercepted a large formation of raiders that
was approaching Portsmouth at 15,000ft. On this occasion Ferdie was
flying as Red 2. However, 152 was re-vectored to 4,000ft where the
enemy formation was spotted 4 miles south of the Isle of Wight:

Red 2 attacked a Ju 87 above and rear and gave short burst at close
range. He saw Ju 87 hit water at speed and turn over. Rounds fired:
640 1-2-3 secs 100-150yds.

Ferdie was remembered by Pilot Officer Roger Hall:

F/O Ferdie was usually known as the 'Bull'. He was small,
unassuming and balding. He was past thirty and been an instructor
in the early days of the war. For this reason, his flying was exact and
if at times he gave the impression that he was being foolhardy it was
only one's ignorance and inexperience which made one think so.

The Bull was an expert in all forms of bad weather flying and if
one were fortunate enough to be flying with him in bad weather
there was never any reason to feel apprehensive. Ferdie always got
back to base somehow. In action, he was cool and calculating but not
a fire eater. And I think his comparative caution was due not to any
lack of aggressiveness but to a studious and analytical turn of mind.

On 21 August, he claimed a 'shared' Ju 88. On 7 October, he led the
squadron against an enemy formation of thirty Ju 88s with a fighter
escort of Me 110s and Me 109s. The enemy aircraft were flying at
17,000ft with 152 Squadron 3,000ft above them. The latter attacked in
line astern.

Firing at the nearest enemy aircraft, after a second pass, he saw white
smoke streaming from two of the bombers. He then climbed to 23,000ft
over Dorchester and saw two Me 109s above him. He climbed after
them into the sun but they were nowhere to be seen.

A poem was written for Ferdie during his time on the squadron
following an incident when his Spitfire was believed to have been
attacked by the IRA. Sadly the author is not known:

Above: Standing in front of one of 152 Squadron's Spitfires are, left to right, Ian Bayles, Richard Inness, P/O Pooch (on the wing), Graham Cox and Ferdie Holmes. (Author's Collection)

Ferdie Holmes was flying
In his Spitfire bright
All went well til engine
Suddenly took fright.

Down came Ferdie earthwards.
Looking for a perch.
Scanned the green sward closely
In his hurried search.

Crashed the dear old Spitfire
Doomed to fly no more
Glancing round he spotted
Poultry by the score.

Ah! Said Ferdie smiling
Here's the place for me
Praps I'll now be getting
Boiled eggs for my tea.

Above: The same group as the previous photograph. Note the parachute lying ready on the wing. (Author's Collection)

Farmer feeding chickens
Soon hove into sight
"You all right young fellow?"
"Yes said Ferdie. Quite.

Off the farmer ambled
Never turned a hair.
Leaving Ferdie standing
Turning blue the air!

Ambulance and tender
Soon drove up all hot.
Bursting to be busy.
Corpse though found they not.

Weak-kneed chicken
Soon they saw instead.
Gave it special treatment
Went and left it dead.

Ends our little ditty
Moral just this one
Never crash a Spitfire
In a chicken run!

(With apologises to a distinguished pilot, much devoted to his feathered friends! Plane sabotaged by the IRA.)

Ferdie left the squadron in 1941 to carry out instructional duties. He returned to an operational unit with 487 RNZAF Squadron in 1944. On 4 December 1944, he was flying Mosquito HR197 from RAF Thorny Island on a night sortie on railway communications in the Ruhr. His aircraft was shot down by anti-aircraft fire and crashed at Haesselte, Germany. He and his navigator, Flying Officer Wilkie Christopherson, were both killed. He was buried in Reichswald Forest War Cemetery near Cleve, Germany. He is remembered by his family, referring to him by the well-known quotation, 'He who takes the greatest risk gets the highest prize'.

HUMPHREYS, Pilot Officer Peter Harry No.84961

Peter was born at Lymington in the New Forest in Hampshire on 1 May 1920. He was the youngest of three brothers. He was educated at Peter Symonds School, Winchester. He was working in a firm of surveyors in 1938 when he enlisted in the RAFVR, being called to full-time service on the outbreak of war.

Peter carried out his training at 5 Initial Training Wing, Hastings,

Left: Pilot Officer Peter Humphreys.
(Courtesy of the Humphreys family)

before moving on to 18 EFTS at Fair Oaks, Chobham, Surrey, and, lastly, 5 FTS at Sealand. He completed his conversion to the Spitfire Mk I at 7 OTU, RAF Hawarden, in September 1940.

Having been commissioned as a pilot officer on 7 September 1940, Peter was posted to 152 Squadron on 29 September. There is little mention of his operational flying during the remaining period of the Battle of Britain, though he certainly took part in some of the worst aerial combats that the squadron experienced during that time.

Pilot Officer Norman Hancock wrote the following: I knew Peter well, sadly he started to get in with a bit of a wrong crowd and we grew apart. The last time I saw him he was getting on a train due to him being posted. He turned and said we must meet up again, but we never did.

Peter remained with the squadron until 1941, moving with it to RAF Portreath, Cornwall. He was then posted to 92 Squadron, which was based at RAF Biggin Hill, Kent, in mid-1941.

In November 1941, he was posted to HQ Middle East, followed a month later with a posting to 112 Squadron at Sidi Heneish, as a flight commander. On 24 April 1942, he was sent to the Fighter School at El Ballah, as an instructor.

He re-joined 92 Squadron on 3 March, then at Castel Benito. He claimed a Me 109 on 7 March. He took command of the squadron on 6 May, and led it through Malta, Sicily and Italy. Peter was awarded the DFC on 1 October 1943. The announcement in *The London Gazette* stated:

> This officer has commanded his squadron since May, 1943, and has led it with great skill and determination. During this period the squadron has destroyed at least 8 enemy aircraft, and Squadron Leader Humphreys has destroyed 2 of these, assisted in the destruction of another and damaged 4 more. This officer is a resourceful pilot whose example has been a great inspiration to others.

After taking command of 111 Squadron, flying the Spitfire Mk.IX, followed by staff duties in Italy, Peter returned to the UK on 1 November 1945, where he was posted to 5 OTU. This unit was soon disbanded and he was posted to HQ 12 Group.

On 11 November 1947, Peter was flying as a passenger on board one of six Lancasters of 115 Squadron taking part in a fighter affiliation exercise. A de Havilland Hornet of 19 Squadron, PX284, was undertaking a mock attack on the Lancaster Peter was in, TW647, when disaster struck. The pilot of the Hornet broke away too late and the two aircraft collided.

The Hornet lost part of a wing in the collision and crashed, its pilot being killed. TW647 broke in two, with only the pilot able to bale-out. The other five men on board were all killed.

Peter was 27 years-old and was cremated at Bournemouth Crematorium.

INNESS, Flying Officer Richard Frederick
No.41292

Richard was born on 4 January 1918 in Calcutta, India. At the age of $4^1/_2$ he came to the UK. He was educated at Aldenham School, Elstree, Hertfordshire. He joined the RAF on a short service commission on 1 August 1938. He carried out his training and after seeing a Spitfire fly in 1939 at Lee-On-Solent, he knew that he wanted to become a fighter pilot.

Richard remembers how difficult it was to be accepted for Fighter Command: 'You had to write into the Air Ministry every month to join Fighter Command; if you missed a month your application would be placed in the pile for an extra month.'

Eventually his application was accepted and Richard successfully completed his conversion to Spitfires and joined 152 Squadron at Acklington in February 1940. He moved south with the squadron and it was not long before he was in aerial combat with the Luftwaffe.

On 25 July, while flying as Red 2, he engaged a large enemy formation over Portland at 11,000ft:

> P/O Inness attacked Me 109 from above and quarter, when rounds were seen entering the fuselage of the E/A. He broke away and climbed after E/A for 2,000ft firing again at 100yds. E/A dived vertically down, but P/O Inness had to take evasive action when 2 Me 109s came on his tail. Rounds fired: 150

He was credited with a 'damaged' following this engagement.

Richard was given the nickname of 'Lord Chumley'. This came about during the time the squadron was stationed at Acklington, when some of the pilots, on 'Release' from readiness, were relaxing in The Sun Hotel in Walkworth, Northumberland. 'We were playing table tennis when this portly colonel type came in and someone asked who he might be.' Recalled Richard. 'I blasted out that it was probably Lord Cholmondeley de la Bottomley, pronounced Chumley de la Bumley. And since then the name Lord Chumley stuck with me throughout my service career.'

On 13 August, while the squadron was in combat over Portland, Richard singled out a Me 110 – he observed hits on the raider's starboard engine and it soon began to belch black smoke with pieces falling from the aircraft. The 110 was last seen losing height into cloud.

However, because he had been concentrating on his attack on the Me 110, Richard did not notice another enemy aircraft move in behind him. He later recalled:

> I was concentrating on the aircraft I was firing at but when I heard a smash on the instrument panel I realised something must be behind and it was a 110. I carried out this steep turn to get out of his sights and he cleared off up into the sun and I travelled home.
>
> Halfway home I felt something cold on my wrist. I looked and it was blood. So, I realised a bullet must have come through the armoured plating hit my arm and finished up in my instrument panel. I made it back to base fortunately. Yep very lucky.
>
> My arm did not start to hurt until at least half hour after it occurring. But at the time I did not know it had happened until I felt something cold on my wrist. The bullet had hit my bone and damaged the tendons that cover the elbow. When I landed I was fairy stiff in that arm and I was not fit enough to fly, so they whisked me down to the Palace Hotel at Torquay, Devon which was a RAF Hospital. I saw a doctor and he said to me 'so you can't move it eh? Let's have a look.' With that he pushed it and I nearly passed out. But it did the trick and I was back on duty the next day …
>
> It was strange on that day; one of my ground crew placed a small set of wings on my instrument panel as a good luck charm. Also, if I remember correctly, it was the day that our Spitfires had been fitted with armoured plating behind the pilot's seat.

On 25 September, Richard took-off as part of 'A' Flight, flying as Red 2, to patrol over the aerodrome as three enemy aircraft were reported in the vicinity. They took up a search formation but were bounced by

Above: Pilot Officer Richard Inness. (Author's Collection)

Me 109s. The Spitfires immediately broke formation. When he levelled out, Richard could see no other aircraft in the sky and returned to base.

The next day he was again in action with nine Spitfires intercepting a large formation of enemy aircraft consisting of an estimated thirty Ju 88s and a fighter escort. Richard was flying as Red 3:

> Red section went into line astern then Echelon starboard and attacked the formation from beam out of the sun in a shallow dive.

140

Sweeping the E/A from front to rear. Other Spitfires also attacked this formation at the same time from above and to the rear. The section made a second attack and 3 Ju 88s were seen to fall away from the formation with smoke belching from them. One crashed on the I. Of Wight and the other two went into the sea several miles south of the I. Of Wight.

On 15 September, the squadron was called to readiness at 04.00 hours as there were reports of a German invasion. The following is Pilot Officer Roger Hall's account from the time they had all arrived at the squadron dispersal hut armed with their pistols:

The arrival of Chumley, the last on the scene, completed the farce. Chumley came through the door of the hut still in his pyjamas his RAF overcoat wrapped round him and his battered hat on his head but back to front. He looked like a German Sailor. Under his arm, he carried his underclothes and uniform. His opening remark – 'What the bloody hell goes on around here? – bastard batman pulling me out of bed in the middle of the night' was drowned by a burst of spontaneous laughter and applause.

Cocky got up from his bed and pulled Chumley's hat off while Dimmy unwrapped his overcoat. The bundle of clothing fell to the ground leaving little Chumley standing in his pyjamas in the middle of the hut while the applause reached a crescendo. The C.O., who seemed equally amused, made some unavailing effort to impress Chumley with the seriousness of the occasion by saying. 'Come on your Lordship if we get a scramble, as we probably will, there's an invasion on you know, you'll bloody well have to take off in your pyjamas.' 'Yes sir, I'll do just that' Chumley replied.

Pilot Officer Roger Hall also remembered an occasion when Richard had to make a force-landing after being attacked by two enemy fighters:

Suddenly I noticed black smoke coming from Chumley's machine and I thought at first his engine was on fire. The smoke was sweeping past my own aircraft and instinctively I looked to see what was behind us. But there was nothing. 'Christ I'm on fire!' Was all that came from Chumley as he realised his predicament. He was apparently throttling his engine back for I could see the blades of his prop slow down and finally stop altogether. I felt a sensation of horror for an instant expecting to see Chumley's machine burst into flames at any moment and drew back some distance behind him. I seemed unable to say anything to him on the R/T thinking that nothing I could say would be of any use.

Chumley pulled his aircraft round in a shallow turn to starboard slowing down considerably as he went. His propeller was quite still. I expected to see him bale out and hoped he would. The smoke seemed to get a little less severe so his engine must be cooling off. 'I'm going to make for Tangmere Roger,' I heard him say, and saw him dive his machine out of the turn and in the direction of Tangmere which was some way to the east of Southampton water.

'Are you O.K?' I replied. 'Oil pipe's gone for a Burton,' he told me. I said I would stick around until he got down lower.

When he had got down to five thousand feet the smoke from Chumley's machine had all but stopped and he was now above the aerodrome at Tangmere manoeuvring into a position for a forced-landing. I stayed at five thousand feet and watched him land which he did with wheels down and get out of the aircraft. From where I was, I could see a lot of smoke coming from the forward part of the aircraft now it had come to rest but the crash tenders and fire engines were already on the scene and were spraying foam all over it.

Richard remembers a typical squadron scramble:

You got up in the morning [and] your batman brought you a cup of tea. You opened the window and said, 'They will be here again'. It [seemed that] everyday was a lovely day, and in fact it was a lovely summer. Unfortunately it was not for us because we were up there in our aircraft.

One would sit around all day reading, sleeping, or messing about and … then 'Scramble! The Spits were dispersed so if a bloke came down with a machine gun firing he couldn't line them all up and hit the lot. So you took off, climbed and then flattened out – you're in bright sunlight up there.

Sweep around; your eyes are looking everywhere – you're watching out. Then suddenly somebody says over the R/T 'Watch out, 6 o'clock above' that's all you properly heard.

Above: The author pictured with Richard Inness. (Author's Collection)

On 25 September, Richard took-off as part of 'A' Flight, flying as Red 2. They were to patrol over the aerodrome due to reports of three enemy aircraft in the vicinity. They took up a search formation and carried on with their patrol.

A number of Me 109s soon bounced the flight from behind and they immediately broke formation going in all directions. After the initial confusion of the combat, on recovering his aircraft Richard levelled out to discover that he was suddenly alone in the sky. He turned for home landing safely back at RAF Warmwell.

Richard once recalled the following:

> I remember the amount of times the radar people were wrong. I was flying with Bottle once. I went up with him – I don't know why, as I was a senior Flight Commander by then.
>
> They sent us both up and I think it was over the Isle of Wight; we got about halfway at about 15,000ft and control called up: 'Return to

base and join Squadron, very many bandits approaching from the south.' Bloody silly – 350 it turned out to be.

It was a raid on Portsmouth. We turned back and found that the squadron had already taken off. So we joined up with them and we went off to battle again. Get in, fire get out and keep doing that as long as you can. It's no good staying around too long because you will have what happened to me when the bullet went through my armoured plating and my arm. You must never stay still.

On 27 September, the squadron scrambled to intercept a large formation of enemy aircraft, which consisted of an estimated forty Ju 88s with a fighter escort of Me 109s. Flying south over Bristol, Richard, as Red 2, destroyed a Me 109.

Richard left the squadron around Christmas-time 1940, commenting that they were 'very happy days, we got up there and just did the task in hand'. He was posted to 53 OTU at Heston, as an instructor and was promoted to flight lieutenant on arrival. He went on to command 130 Squadron from October 1943 to February 1944, and then commanded 222 Natal Squadron until June of that year. He left the RAF in 1946, having attained the rank of squadron leader.

JONES, Pilot Officer John Sinclair Bucknall No.33467

John was born on 17 February 1919 in Marlborough, Wiltshire. He was the only son of Group Captain J.H.O. Jones and Charlotte M.G. Jones. He was educated at Canford School, Dorset. He entered RAF College Cranwell in January 1938 as an Honorary King's Cadet, winning the R.M. Groves Memorial prize

Left: Pilot Officer John Jones.
(Courtesy of the Jones family)

Above: Pilot Officer John Jones' Spitfire at dispersal. (Courtesy of the Jones family)

Below: Pilot Officer John Jones relaxing with P/O Pooch. (Courtesy of the Jones family)

Above: Pilot Officer John Jones with Acting Station Officer Jill. (Courtesy of the Jones family)

for being the best all round pilot of his intake. He completed his training and was commissioned in October 1939 and the same month joined 152 Squadron then based at Acklington.

While on a routine patrol over the North Sea on 27 February, flying as No.2 to Pilot Officer Timothy Wildblood, he helped in shooting down a He 111 10 miles east of Coquet Island, Northumberland. He watched the enemy bomber fall towards the sea, hoping to see the crew bale-out which they did. He radioed their position so a rescue launch could pick them up. Sadly, by the time the rescue launch arrived at the location all the crew had drowned. John was present at the burial of these German airmen and was a pall-bearer for one of the airmen's coffins.

On 25 July, flying as Black 1, with Sergeant Denis Robinson as Black 2, John engaged a number of Me 109s below him:

> Fired short burst with full deflection at 150yds. Black smoke issued from enemy, which turned sharply left and down. Fired further long burst at 50yds with slight deflection. Enemy broke up behind

Another portrait of Pilot Officer John Jones. (Courtesy of the Jones family)

147

Above: Pilot Officer John Jones (on the left) and his friend Pilot Officer Doug Shepley on Warmwell's airfield roller. (Courtesy of the Jones family)

---

cockpit and rolled onto its side pouring smoke thickly. It was seen to plunge vertically into the sea 3-5 miles south of Portland. Rounds fired: 2,110

John was credited with one 'confirmed' and one 'probable' for this combat. He went on to be involved in many of the heaviest aerial combat engagements during the months of July and the beginning of August.

Like most pilots, John was physically and mentally exhausted at the end of a day of aerial combat. On landing one day after a sortie, instead of slowing down and turning into his pen, he continued taxiing at speed, only stopping when he hit the airfield's perimeter hedge. The rescue crews raced towards his stricken Spitfire believing he was injured. But when they pulled open John's cockpit hood they found him sound asleep. Granted four days' leave, John headed to the family home, 'Holylake', on the Wirral. He slept for the whole first day of this period.

Above: Pilot Officer John Jones (on the left) with his friend Pilot Officer Doug Shepley. Both men would be killed in action in the same month. (Courtesy of the Jones family)

Above: A picture of Pilot Officer John Jones' Spitfire with a prayer written on it. (Courtesy of the Jones family)

On 11 August, four aircraft of Red and Yellow sections took-off to patrol over Portland. John was flying as Yellow 2 in Spitfire R6614, with Flight Lieutenant Derek Boitel-Gill as Yellow 1. The formation was bounced by Me 109s from behind with cannon rounds hitting John's aircraft:

> Yellow 1 saw 2 Me 109s 500 feet above him so climbed up and was able to fire two short bursts at 500yds and closing to 200yds but without any apparent result. He saw Yellow 2 going down but the pilot jumped out and the parachute opened.

Flight Lieutenant Derek Boitel-Gill circled around John as he was descending on his parachute to protect him from enemy fighters. He reported John's position, which was about 10 miles off Swanage. The local lifeboat was sent out to pick him up, but when arriving in the area John could not be found. Squadron aircraft also took-off to search the area where John had baled-out. It is believed that he must have been badly injured from the enemy fire and was not strong enough to stay

150

67: Hauptmann Armin Ettling of 7/JG2. Ettling was credited with shooting down Pilot Officer John Jones. This image is believed to have been taken on Ettling's return from his combat sortie on 11 August. (Courtesy of Erik Mombeeck)

Pilot Officer John Jones' Commonwealth War Graves Commission headstone. (Courtesy of the CWGC)

afloat in the sea. It is believed that he was badly injured and, with the added to the weight of his parachute, he drowned.

Three of the squadron's Spitfires, as well as Blenheims from 604 Squadron, were desptached to carry out a search and rescue mission, but without success. One of the last people who saw John alive was one of his aircraft's mechanics who remembered well that fateful day:

> We were at 30 minutes standby and most of the pilots were down at the mess, Mr Jones was fiddling about with his car, a sports car, I believe it was dark green. The car was parked near the dispersal crew hut and the phone rang. Mr Jones shouted 'I'll get it', I was working on the engine of aircraft V when he came running out shouting 'Start up'.
>
> I started the engine of his aircraft, which was coded R, while he was putting his 'chute on. I helped him strap in and he said, 'Get the rest of the pilots'. He taxied out and took off and never came back.
>
> Mr Jones' car stood at the dispersal hut for some time after he went missing and I believe his mother came and took it away.

There is the possibility that John did actually survive his parachute descent. At a point some 30 miles off the French coast, a Heinkel He 59b floatplane, *werk nummer* 1845, was spotted by 604 Squadron's Squadron Leader Anderson and Pilot Officer Crew at 13.35 hours. A rescue aircraft from Seenotzentrale Cherbourg, the He 59, was on the water picking up downed airmen. Air Ministry orders stated that these aircraft were to be destroyed, it being thought that they were carrying out reconnaissance missions over the British coast and convoys underway at sea. The Blenheim duly attacked and destroyed the floatplane, which promptly sank. It is possible that John may have been on this aircraft having just being picked up.

Some days later John's body was washed up at Yport on the French coast. He was initially buried by the Germans in Yport Cemetery on 11 September 1940. After the war his body was re-interred at Sainte Marie Cemetery, Le Havre, on 25 June 1947.

John had joined the RAF to fly as this was his passion in life, though, as he had made clear to his family during one period of leave, he was not comfortable shooting down other airmen: 'I have to think I am not shooting down the person in the flying helmet but shooting down the machine.'

His good friends at the squadron were Pilot Officer Shepley and Pilot Officer Timothy Wildblood, all three would be killed in combat during August 1940.

The following poem was written by John's mother:

My little boy
Who I loved so much,
Who lays in my arms
And smiled at me,
So cosy, so warm,
How lovely to touch!

And now it is just
Your photo I see
In the little St. John
You left in your drawer.
And here on the earth
Is that all to me?

I've travelled alone,
Yet never alone,
Through the years of war,
For five long years,
And because of your deeds
The war has been won,
But as Churchill said
With Blood Sweat and tears!

But today we are free,
And the world lives on,
And over London
A pageant flies,
To show the speed
And types of machines,
The progress of flight,
And how it was done.

And I stand beneath
In Trafalgar Square

With a new little man,
Your sister's child.
His father had gone
But he hardly knows,
The planes sweep over,
The crowd goes wild.

And I show him the planes,
And tell him of deeds,
And we smile at it all.
While my heart just bleeds.

KEARSEY, Sergeant Albert Wallace
No.60518

Albert was born on 26 October 1916. He was educated at Cheltenham Grammar School. In the mid-1930s, 'Bill', as he was more commonly known, enlisted into the RAF Reserve as a Class 'F' Airman u/t pilot 700510.

In September 1939, he was called-up for full-time service and carried out his training at 5 FTS. After completing his training in December of that year he became a staff pilot at 10 Bombing and Gunnery School, which was then based at RAF Warmwell, carrying out practice sorties on the nearby range at Chesil Beach close to Portland. After Spitfire conversion at 7 OTU Hawarden, he was posted to 152 Squadron in mid-September 1940 as a replacement pilot due to heavy losses the squadron had suffered in July and August. Bill arrived on the squadron having amassed no less than 447 hours and thirty-five minutes flying time on a variety of types, more than most young pilots who fought in the Battle of Britain.

On 30 September, flying as Green 2 in Spitfire K9840, Bill and the rest of the squadron engaged a large formation of Me 109s and Me 110s over the aerodrome:

Green 2 (Sgt Kearsey) was weaving above Squadron and when it turned to attack he made a surprise attack on Bf 110 and closed to 50 yards. Enemy aircraft turned over on its back and dived vertically. Green 1 saw this aircraft go down in flames in the vicinity of Chesil Bank or off the west of Fleet.

Bill's personal account of this engagement adds to his claim:

> I think it was the raid on Westland's Aircraft at Yeovil, one of them. Anyway, we were scrambled and after a bit I spotted them but couldn't get anyone's attention. I dived after these 110s five of them. Now's my chance, I thought, but opened fire too soon out of range and they scattered.
>
> I kept after one but by the time it started to go down I had used all my ammunition. I lost sight of it – too much else going on. But Dudley saw it hit the sea off Chesil beach. It was really an awful shambles when we were up there. We just went for the nearest enemy plane and let him have all we had. Very little was known about fighter tactics in those early days.
>
> The most frustrating thing of all was to see some of the enemy aircraft limping home while we were refuelling on the ground.

In a similar manner, Bill remembered one particular aerial combat over Portland:

> Nothing prepares you for your first combat. It's the need to react instantly like nothing else. My first time? I remember well this is alright. Then suddenly a voice over the intercom yells 'Break to Port go!' And everyone was gone. Just as I was wondering what the hell to do, bars of smoke began appearing all around me and looking up in the mirror I saw a Me 109 with winking lights along its wings. Christ! I was being shot at and I wrenched the controls and the Spit was falling and vibrating like mad. I thought 'God I've been shot down'.
>
> I must have lost ten thousand feet and thinking I should bale out. It occurred to me to centralise the controls and the Spit, being the beautiful forgiving aircraft it is, came out of the spin and flew gracefully on.
>
> I looked around. The sky was empty. I hadn't been hit. I hadn't shot anything down. I hadn't even fired my guns. I was so ashamed that, just between the two of us, I fired a quick burst into the sea off Portland. But when I landed they seemed quite pleased to see me, surprised perhaps. 'Cheer up' they said, 'tomorrow when we go up we'll have a pilot who will know what to expect, and who will be ready for the call to break.' And I was!

Sergeant Bill Kearsey. (Courtesy of the Kearsey family)

Sometimes the German R/T frequencies would cross ours, and as we saw them we'd hear a frantic German's voice yelling 'Achtung Spitfeur!' It sounded just like a bad war film.

The 109s? They were good, a good aircraft and their tactics were much more developed than ours. But they were often operating near the limit of their range, they couldn't stay long – and they couldn't stay with you in a turn. And how a Spit could turn.

Bill described typical operations with the squadron:

We flew in formation with a Tail-end Charlie weaving at the back to keep a look out. Sometimes we all got back to find the poor bugger had been picked off by a couple of 109s and nobody even noticed. But I used to volunteer to be tail-ender. I hated being up in formation, preferred to weave about and keep a good look out. I found I could always see them coming.

Once I got separated from my section and was attacked by a pair of 109s. I began turning hard but just as I was getting behind the first one the second came in behind me. They were coming in on interlocking circles so that just as I was getting close to a firing position on one the other would be coming in and I'd have to break-off and out turn him, clever stuff, now what? I just kept turning and sweating and praying and cursing. Then I saw they were getting out of sequence and I managed to get in a squirt and he spun towards the sea and the other one dived away at once.

At the time, I thought he was shamming, hoping I'd follow, but now I'm not sure about a sucker trick like that after all the clever stuff. I've flown back over the sea after an engagement and spotted as many as ten patches of florazine in the water and nobody claimed a thing.

For the pilots, boredom was immense while waiting at dispersal and things had to be found to do. We had this top hat known as the 'Hyderabad hat'. People would wear it at celebrations or playing poker for luck etc. One afternoon being at a loose end we decided we'd try and bag a couple of pheasants. Cocky was wearing the 'Hyderabad hat' and we'd already shot one pheasant when a chap turned up who looked like the landowner. I said quick hide the bird somewhere, and Cocky stuffed the bird in the hat and put it on his head. Anyway the chap was a gent, and just chatted for a while. [He]

Above: Sergeant Bill Kearsey pictured standing next to UM-N. (Author's Collection)

never asked why an RAF officer was wearing a top hat or why two long tails feathers were sticking out the back.

On 14 November, Blue section engaged a lone Ju 88 over Poole. Pilot Officer Marrs was flying as Blue 1, with Bill as Blue 2:

2 Spitfires, blue section 152 Squadron up Warmwell 0908 hours 14/11/40 down 0945 hours. When at 15,000ft saw condensation trails at 20/25,000ft heading north. When west of Shaftsbury section came up on Ju 88 at 24,000ft. Blue 1 made 3 attacks from left and right quarters and then Blue 2 attacked from the beam and from the quarter to astern. Blue 2 continued the attack until the whole machine was on fire the port engines having caught fire after the first attack. E/A crashed and exploded near Bournemouth.

Once again, Bill has left us with his own description of this engagement:

I was flying as No.2 to Boy Marrs and they brought us out of cloud right on the beam of this Ju 88 about a mile away. A very good

Above: Sergeant Bill Kearsey flying on dawn patrol over Portland. (Author's Collection)

controller. Boy went in first but then broke away. I called on the R/T are you alright? But the response sounded confused. I thought he had been hit. I was so angry I just kept on firing and I was still pressing the tit after the ammunition had run out. Bits were falling off the 88 by then and it crashed into the side of a house in Poole.

Boy came on the R/T and said he'd stopped one right in the windscreen which had gone completely opaque. He couldn't see a thing foreword [sic] so he closed in tight and landed in formation, he touched down as I did.

He said it was my 88 though he could have claimed half at least, but Boy was like that. Great to have him as my section leader. He was only nineteen.

On release, we drove over to Poole to see if there were any souvenirs to be had. The Army were there clearing up. Someone said this is the bloke who shot it down and an older Army officer asked if I would like to see the bodies of the crew? Perhaps he was irritated we'd left them to clear up.

Before I could say anything, he pulled back a tarpaulin, and the Germans were young men indistinguishable from us. Grim. They gave me a small French automatic one of them had in his pocket. The barrel and sleeve had been damaged by the impact. Then I went home, had a drink, went to bed and spent the worst night of my life.

Bill's wife once recalled many of the characters who served on the squadron, as well as the stress and anxiety of waiting for the day when she would hear that her husband had been killed in action:

How people saw them, we all knew they were fighting for us and that we mustn't lose. They seemed to be surrounded by a kind of aura at least to us lesser mortals! It was almost impossible for Bill to buy himself a drink in those days. They'd see those wings and it would be, 'What'll you have boy'. I was embarrassed sometimes.

They were wonderful company, always cheerful, made light of everything. I don't think I've had so much fun. But they were still very young boys almost, especially when they'd had lots to drink and the evening got a bit boisterous. Sometimes the sirens would sound but we never took cover. They would rush out into the dark to watch and climb up on their cars to get a better view and laugh. (One night the bombs were overhead but the bombs seemed to be dropping in the fields and they kept saying silly things like 'What do you think they're aiming at?' 'You would think it's England'. And they'd wave and shout 'We're over here'. And somebody said, 'I think they're digging for victory. Then often they called out 'Go home you're assisting the enemy!' Silly things like that. How could you be afraid when you were with people like that. I never was. I found the bombing exciting, I suppose I shouldn't have.

One afternoon, coming back to my local hotel, I saw two officers waiting outside. I thought, 'Oh, this is it', and I walked away. I walked around Dorchester for ages. I couldn't go back to the hotel – but when I did they were gone.

Sometimes when I'd go out I would look up at the sky and see the planes turning high up. You would hear the engines and the sound of the machine guns and you'd wonder if it was them. And sometimes a plane would fall away and fall and fall and you'd hope it wasn't one of ours. Time and time again someone would go, but the next night there they would all be, drinks in their hands and carefree. Apparently something else that courage was I suppose.

Bill left 152 Squadron in 1941, being commissioned on 22 January 1941. He went on to serve with Bomber Command throughout his remaining service. He was released from the RAF in 1946, with the rank of flight lieutenant, joining the RAFVR in April 1948.

Bill's brother Philip also served in the Battle of Britain but was lost off Malta in 1941. Bill passed away in October 1993. He had once commented, 'the important thing was to see them coming, it was the one you didn't see that got you'.

KLEIN, Sergeant Zygmunt
No.780685

Zygmunt was born on 24 August 1918 in his home country of Poland. Little is known of him before he arrived in the UK in early 1940, following the German occupation of Poland. He joined the RAF in February that year. He told his family when he left Poland, 'I have to go, I must shoot down a few Germans.'

After his initial training and conversion to Spitfires, he was posted to 234 Squadron on 6 August 1940, this unit being based at RAF Middle Wallop. Zygmunt destroyed a Me 109 on 7 August 1940 and a Me 110 'shared' on 4 September. While with 234 Squadron, he met a fellow Polish pilot named Sergeant Josef Szlagowski, and they soon became good friends.

On 5 October both pilots were posted to 152 Squadron and it was quickly noticed that the two young airmen were inseparable. Both men hated all Germans, and when they returned from a sortie they would enquire if any PoWs had been brought into the station guardroom. If so, they would attempt to see the prisoners, at which point the two pilots would ask where they were from. Any reply was met with the comment from 'Ziggy' and Josef that that place would be targeted that night by the RAF. They were soon banned from any contact with prisoners.

On 26 November, Ziggy crash-landed his Spitfire, Mk I L1048, near Torquay after running out of fuel. Josef waited back at Warmwell anxiously for his friend's safe return. He was relieved when a message was received saying Ziggy was safe and had crash-landed, as the Squadron ORB points out:

Zygmunt Klein beside his Spitfire. (Author's Collection)

Above left: Leutnant Rudolf Pflanz, 1/JG 2. Above right: Major Helmut Wick.
(both Author's Collection)

While on patrol in the afternoon Sgt. Pilot Klein, one of our Polish pilots was reported missing. After some time a message was received that he had crash landed near Torquay owing to [a] lack of petrol. He was unhurt and his 'plane not so badly damaged as might be expected. His companion in the patrol flight missed him first while near Portland. It was a great relief to all when the news arrived that Sgt. Klein was safe. It was quite dark when this news was received.

Ziggy was fondly remembered by Sergeant Bill Kearsey's wife:

We would all go to somewhere in the country or to Weymouth or Bournemouth in the evenings. If there was a band I would dance with them. They would buy me drinks, even though I couldn't possibly keep up with them.

I remember one evening looking up and seeing all my drinks lined up all different colours and I thought 'Oh help I've had enough' and Bill was nowhere in sight. But Zig must have noticed and he came over. He stood and made a little bow and said, 'Mrs Kearsey, may I have the honour to escort you to your hotel'. Rescued!

Zig looked the romantic idea of a Polish aristocrat to every girl who saw him and I believe he took full advantage of it. But he was always very correct and considerate with me. His charm worked on many ladies and he became very fond of a young WAAF while at Warmwell.

On 28 November, flying as Green 3, Ziggy was not so lucky. At a height of 22,000ft, vapour trails were seen from the south and these turned out to be an estimated twenty Me 109s. Soon the Spitfires were attacked by these aircraft, with 152 Squadron breaking in all directions. Ziggy immediately dropped into a dive and turned to follow his No.1, Pilot Officer 'Boy' Marrs. They went into attack a Me 109, but Marrs had to break off as his windscreen was covered with oil from his own aircraft.

Ziggy did not survive the engagement: His death was witnessed by Pilot Officer Ferdie Holmes and Flying Officer Geoffery Baynham:

> I saw a Spitfire spinning three or four times over the sea before disappearing from sight. I was flying at 22,000ft and when I was climbing to intercept a Me 109 I saw a Spitfire spin down from a formation of seven or eight Me 109s and I think this must have been Ziggy. I could not watch it any longer owing to the pressure of enemy aircraft.

It is believed he was shot down by Leutnant Rudolf Pflanz, Stab 1/Jageschwader 2. Ziggy was flying Spitfire P9427. He was 22 years of age and had completed twenty-eight combat sorties and sixty-five operational flights during his time in Britain. The Squadron ORB: 'It appears that we have lost a very gallant pilot and ally.'

MARRS, Pilot Officer Eric Simcox
No.33572

Eric was born on 9 July 1921 in Dover, Kent. He was educated at Dauntsey's School, Wiltshire. He joined the RAF in April 1939 and was

Above: Pilot Officer 'Boy' Marrs sitting in his Spitfire, *Old Faithful*. (Courtesy of Tim Watson)

accepted as a flight cadet at RAF Cranwell. On completion of his training he was commissioned on 7 March 1940.

Eric joined 152 Squadron on 17 March 1940. He was only 19 years of age at the time and he soon, somewhat predictably, acquired the nickname 'Boy'.

Extracts from Eric's letters were published in *Aeroplane* magazine in 1945. They included a description of an action on the afternoon of 13 August when he was with nine other 152 Squadron aircraft that engaged an enemy formation over Portland harbour:

> We climbed up to 15,000ft over Portland, soon we were told over the R/T 'Many enemy aircraft approaching Portland from the south.' About two minutes later I had my first sight of them, a cloud of black specks milling around and around.
>
> We climbed up another 3,000ft up sun of them and about five miles south of Portland, and they were there. There must have been more than hundreds of them, Ju 87s escorted by Bf 110s. I must say

the sight of all these aircraft made my heart sink, how could ten Spitfires stop all these? However, we were ordered into line astern and down we came out of the sun straight behind the bombers. That dive cheered me up no end.

I was going too fast to get a good shot in; I shall know better next time. I nipped under them at the last minute and went down in a dive, I then met up with another Bf 110. I could not help it, there were so many of them, we circled round each other for a bit, each turning to get on the other's tail. But my attention was soon drawn by another Bf 110.

Down underneath him I went and pulled up giving him a long burst into the belly. Nothing seemed to happen. I was then occupied by yet another 110. I milled around with him for a bit, but when I wanted to get a shot in I found I had run out of ammunition. I rolled on my back and pulled out and went home.

This was Eric's first encounter with the enemy. Three days later, on 16 August, he was again in combat following an evening patrol over Portland. The order was given from control to 'pancake' and return to base. Eric tilted his wing and, to his surprise, he spotted two He 111s in the distance. He called up the sector controller on the R/T and reported his sighting. The order was given to attack and the Spitfires dived on the enemy aircraft:

I managed to keep sight of the rear one and when it came out the other side of the thickish mist I was able to shoot it up. I left it with smoke coming from both engines and my own machine covered in oil from it. I don't think it could have got home and I'm pretty sure it didn't.

For this, Eric was credited with a 'probable'. On 18 August, he was one of eleven 152 Squadron aircraft that engaged a formation of some thirty Ju 87s and escorting Me 109s preparing to attack the radar stations in the Solent area. The squadron was vectored to a height of 4,000ft, and a position 4 miles south of the Isle of Wight. The squadron dived in line astern, Eric flying as Black 2:

Black 2 attacked several Ju 87s which took evasive action making steep turns at low speed. Black 2 gave good deflection shots to one

Ju 87 which caught fire at port wings root. Black 2 broke away and saw the Ju 87 dive into the sea. Black 2 continued the attack until his ammunition ran out. He was then attacked by a Me 109 and did steep turns away and then headed for home.

Pilot Officer Dennis Fox-Male fondly remembers 'Boy' in this manner:

He was the most charming boy (of only 20), a brilliant pilot, one of the last of the Cranwell regulars who would undoubtedly have achieved very high rank in the RAF. He was also a lucky pilot. He would come back from a fortnight's leave and intercept a single German bomber on his first or second patrol when no-one had seen a thing while he was away.

On 22 August, Eric claimed a share in the destruction of a Do 17. Three days later, on the night of the 25th, a number of 'time delayed' bombs were dropped on the airfield. Eric remembers the moment one of the bombs exploded: 'It went off just as I was falling to sleep last night, it shook me considerably'.

In early September Eric decided to name his Spitfire *Old Faithful* as it was the oldest aircraft in the squadron and had clocked up over 300 flying hours. Later that month he was to get his next confirmed 'kill'.

On 17 September, he was leading Blue Section on a patrol at 15,000ft over Portland – the other pilots were Sergeant Kenneth Holland and Flying Officer Peter O'Brian. Blue Section was vectored over Shepton Mallet at 17,000ft in an effort to intercept

Above: Cuthbert Orde's drawing of Pilot Officer 'Boy' Marrs. (Courtesy of the RAF Museum)

what was reported as a lone raider. Having then been vectored to 280 degrees a single Ju 88 was sighted flying in a northern direction. The section given the command 'Tally Ho!' by Eric, and it engaged the enemy carrying out a No.1 attack.

The Ju 88 immediately dived for the cover of a bank of clouds at 5,000ft. Eric, flying as Blue 1, fired his guns first, hitting the bomber's radiator and starboard engine. Glycol began to pour from the Ju 88: Its starboard engine emitted white smoke and then stopped altogether. The remaining two aircraft of the section then made their move.

After Eric's initial engagement, however, he noticed fumes coming from his own aircraft:

> During the scrap, I noticed an aerodrome with big runways standing out and showing up well. I made for it and as I was still at about 12,000ft my engine began to shudder very violently, making the whole aerodrome shake. It then seized up solid. I then noticed that the aerodrome was covered with small square concrete blocks to prevent German transport aircraft landing. I had come down and was able to pick a spot more or less free from blocks where I landed without damage to my aircraft. The aerodrome was one just being built and that was the reason for the concrete blocks.

This aerodrome was RAF Colerne. 'I inspected my aircraft and found one bullet hole through my oil cooler, I had lost my oil and my engine had seized up.' The lone Ju 88 crashed at 14.00 hours at Ladywell Barn, three miles from Imber village in Wiltshire.

Eric was credited with a share in the destruction of this Ju 88 – which also features in Holland's and O'Brian's entries in this book. The next day the members of the flight travelled up to visit the wreckage of their victim:

> We arrived about 5 p.m. it was in very good condition and we were extremely interested. We arrived to find quite a crowd all-round the machine, though kept at a distance by a rope. We were able to climb all over it and see where our bullets had gone and I was able to see where I had hit his radiator. We stayed two hours and then pushed on to Salisbury.

One consequence of this combat was that Eric lost his *Old Faithful*, a machine that had got him through all his previous engagements against the Luftwaffe unscathed. *Old Faithful* was repaired and sent to a training squadron.

It is interesting to note that the shooting down of this Ju 88 has a direct link to Marrs' old school, Dauntsey's. Bruce Lewis, a pupil there in the Battle of Britain, recalled what happened:

> We were outside the tuck shop during morning break. A Luftwaffe bomber flew low over the school with a shapely little Spitfire in hot pursuit. Later we learnt that the Spitfire had shot down the Ju 88 near Imber on Salisbury Plain. What really set us boys on fire was the news that the victorious pilot was Eric Marrs, who, not so long ago, had been a pupil at our school. As far as Dauntsey's was concerned, the RAF could not have had a more effective recruiting officer than Marrs![3]

On 25 September, 'B' Flight intercepted a large formation of enemy aircraft over Bath. Squadron Leader Peter Devitt was leading the flight. Eric, flying as Black 2, attacked a Ju 88 but was driven off by Me 110s acting as fighter escort. He then spotted a lone Ju 88 and dived down to attack:

> I put a long burst into it and it also streamed glycol from its starboard engine. My attention was then occupied by a Me 110 which came to help the Heinkel. A steep turn was enough to get behind it as it did not seem very anxious to stay and fight. I came in from the starboard quarter again and kept my finger on the firing button, turning in behind it. Its starboard engine (becoming a habit now) streamed glycol.
>
> Suddenly there was an almighty bang and I broke away quickly. I looked around and glanced at my engine and oil tanks and positioned myself for another attack, this time going for the port engine. I just began to fire when my ammunition petered out.

Though it was a serious offence to carry out any form of victory roll on returning from a sortie, one afternoon Eric did just that over Warmwell:

> On returning, I beat up the dispersal hut and I was in high spirits – but it is strictly verboten and I was seen. I was therefore given four days' duty pilot to cool me off and here I languish having completed

one-and-a-half days of my sentence. Still, it is a good opportunity to read and write some very necessary letters.

Like most pilots during the Battle of Britain, Eric enjoyed an evening out with his fellow pilots, as he recalled:

> The squadron had decided to have a party in celebration of its 60th Hun and we arranged to have it in Swanage come what might. As it happened it was rather unfortunate because we had to drink on empty stomachs. We all missed our lunch and tea due to having to go on 'flaps' and we finally stopped flying about seven. We then all went off finally to Swanage and began drinking cocktails and sherry.
>
> We began at about nine and had an excellent dinner with champagne and port, etc. to accompany it. We then all moved off to another hotel, where we seemed to be able to drink without limitation till an hour of the morning. It actually turned out that the proprietor of this hotel had been registered and was waiting to be called up.
>
> He was therefore selling off all his stock of which he had plenty. His licence had run out and he had not bothered to renew it and he was therefore not very careful as to what hours he kept.
>
> I finally arrived back at camp at about 05:30am to find Dudley Williams 'out' on my bed … We were 'on' at 06:30am in the morning. We both passed out pretty efficiently when we reached dispersal, and even a telephone ringing for half an hour failed to wake us up.

Eric claimed another damaged He 111 during this engagement, a combat that also involved two 609 (West Riding) Squadron pilots, Pilot Officer Agazarian and Pilot Officer Miller, and Pilot Officer Urwin-Mann of 238 Squadron. The victim crashed at Poole, Dorset.

On his return to Warmwell, Eric examined his aircraft and counted eleven bullet holes in it. The one that had caused the loud bang in his cockpit had come along from the rear, nipped in the right-hand side of the fuselage and smashed the socket into which the R/T was plugged.

At 09.40 hours on 27 September 1940, Marrs intercepted a Ju 88A-5, 4U+RL of 3Staffel, Fernaufklarungsgruppe 123. The aircraft's pilot, Feldwebel Helmut Ackenhausen, was an experienced flyer and had flown many operational sorties. The aircraft's mission had been to photograph the dock gates of the Manchester Ship Canal.

Ackenhausen was flying at 23,000ft when 4U+RL was engaged by three Spitfires of 152 Squadron, one of which was flown by Marrs. In the melee that followed, the Ju 88 was hit on its port engine and began to lose height, with the loss of one engine completely. Ackenhausen carried on out over the Bristol Channel before he came to the conclusion that he would be unable to get back to France. Turning back towards land he began looking for a suitable location to land.

The Ju 88 began to glide towards the beach at Porlock, eventually ditching 20 yards off the shoreline. The three Spitfires followed the bomber down, making sure the crew did not set fire to it. Obergefreiter Wilhelm Reuhl, the aircraft's flight engineer, had been killed in the engagement. His body was removed from the wreckage and covered with a blanket on the beach. In time he was buried in the local cemetery at Porlock and still lies there today.

Meanwhile, the surviving members of Ackenhausen's crew, the other two being Oberleutnant Willi Rude (navigator) and Oberfeldwebel Erwin Riehle (wireless operator/gunner), were apprehended by local civilians and a lone naval officer armed only with a pistol. Escorted by a local civilian on horseback, they were taken to Minehead Police Station. They were interned in Canada for the duration of the war.

Dennis Corner was a schoolboy from Porlock:

At the time, I was a schoolboy attending the Minehead County School, now Minehead Middle School. And on that Friday morning I was home in Porlock and, having felt unwell, stayed in bed.

Suddenly I heard planes overhead and people shouting in the streets. I jumped out of bed and looked out of the window. A Spitfire flew over doing a victory roll, as we called it, and people shouted that a German plane was down. Immediately, all thoughts of sickness left me. I jumped into my clothes, left the house and ran into the street with all the others. When I got to the Pound at the top of High Bank I joined Miss Dorothy Ridler of Doverhay Farm, who had arrived at the same moment on her bike. Together we ran across Court Place fields, through the Long Back to the marshes and on to New Works.

We arrived just in time to see three German prisoners come over the top of the beach with several men escorting them. I remember well how they were dressed and wearing forage caps and especially

Above This group, pictured in front of a 152 Squadron Spitfire, comprises, left to right, Sergeant Eric Shepperd, Pilot Officer Roger Hall, Flying Officer Christopher Deanesly, Pilot Officer Arthur Watson, Flight Lieutenant Derek Boitel-Gill, Pilot Officer 'Boy' Marrs, and Flight Lieutenant Peter O'Brian. (Author's Collection)

one very tall man. There was great excitement and I recall old farmer Dave Ridler saying 'They've got 'em.' It was said later that he was waving a pitchfork, but as this was quite a common implement to be carrying in those days that didn't seem to register with me.

Most of the men were workmen who had been building pill boxes 'now demolished' along the beach. I believe only one Englishman was armed and that was a Naval officer who always wore a pistol in a holster. He was in charge of a salvage party which had been salvaging a Fleet Air Arm plane, a Fairey Albacore, which had a fortnight before made a forced-landing on the marsh at Sparkhayes.

The German prisoners walked quietly away across the marsh and were driven away in Mr. Jim Rolland's car together with P.C. Curtis and escorted by Mr Bert Rice on his pony. They were then taken to Minehead Police station. I, and many others went to the top of the beach where we could see the plane lying at low water mark near Redsands. It was a Ju 88 which was a fighter bomber capable of speeds exceeding 300mph, fast for those days.

No one approached the plane as we were told there were unexploded bombs on board. The rear gunner had been killed and his body was brought out later and covered with a blanket and laid on the beach. He was later buried in Porlock cemetery. An army guard was soon at the scene and the tide soon covered the plane.

On Saturday and Sunday people came from miles around and took away parts of the plane for souvenirs. The machine-guns were given to the Minehead School Air Training Corps. I have recently spoken to Mr Andy Hyde who was a Sergeant in the Corps and was responsible for the cleaning and renovating of the guns. These were called 'Rheinmetal borsig' and the boys not only had the guns but ammunition. Like true school boys, Andy and his pals fired a gun from his bedroom window and there are still marks of the tracer bullets on the chimney of the house in Minehead.

Helmut Ackenhausen has also left an account of that day:

I can't say where we met the Spitfires, but immediately my wireless operator warned 'Spitfire below!' Shortly afterwards a hail of machine-gun fire rattled through our aircraft. Our intercom failed and the mechanic/gunner, down below in the ventral cupola, was apparently knocked out in this first attack. Immediately I put the Ju 88 into a dive, making evasive turns at the same time, but my airspeed became so great that I lost control until, at a height of above 10,000ft I was able to level off.

At this height, I expected to get optimum performance from my aircraft, but although I fought back desperately there was no escape. I saw two or three large jagged holes appear in my left wing and the metal skin peeled back like the leaves of a cabbage. At that moment, my port engine failed. I pushed the 88 down into another steep dive, hoping to reach a layer of cloud, with my airspeed again building up to about 340mph. I levelled out in the cloud, trimmed the aircraft for single-engine flight.

Above: Feldwebel Helmut Ackenhausen, seen here second from the left, with his crew. Oberfeldwebel Erwin Riehle can be seen on right.

Below: Feldwebel Helmut Ackenhausen's Ju 88 after its crash-landing on Porlock Beach. (Courtesy Andy Saunders)

The following is taken from Pilot Officer Marrs' (Green 2) Combat Report from 27 September:

> I attacked from the starboard beam. There was return fire from the top rear gun. I closed to about 100yds and broke away again.
>
> I was able to get another good attack on quarter turning behind to rear. The enemy aircraft was now diving for cloud; I fired at him until he disappeared into the cloud. I broke away and waited on the other side.
>
> The remainder of the flight assisted on the bringing down of this aircraft by disabling the engine of the enemy aircraft.

At the beginning of October, Eric was badly injured while intercepting a He 111 over Portland, as he later described:

> Crash, the whole world seemed to be tumbling in on me. I pushed the stick forward hard. Went into a vertical dive and held it until I was below cloud. I had a look around. The chief trouble was that petrol was gushing into the cockpit at the rate of gallons all over my feet and there was sort of a lake of petrol in the bottom of the cockpit. My knee and leg were tingling all over as if I had pushed them into a bed of nettles. There was a bullet hole in my windscreen where a bullet had come in and entered the dashboard knocking away the starter button.
>
> Another bullet I think an explosive one had knocked away one of petrol taps in front of the joystick, spattering my leg with little splinters and sending a chunk of something through the backside of my petrol tank near the bottom. I made for home at top speed to get there before my petrol ran out. I was about fifteen miles from the aerodrome and it was heart-rending business with all that petrol gushing over my legs and constant danger of fire.
>
> About five miles from the drome smoke began to come from under the dashboard. I thought the whole thing might blow up at any minute so I switched off my engine. The smoke stopped and I glided towards the drome and tried putting my wheels down. One came down and the other remained stuck up. I tried to get the one that was down up again, it was stuck down. There was nothing for it but to make a one wheel landing. I switched on the engine again to make the aerodrome. It took me some way and then began to

smoke again so I hastily switched off. I made a good landing touching down lightly. The unsupported wing slowly began to drop. I was able to hold it up for some time and then came down the wing tip on the ground. I began to slew round and counteracted as much as possible with the brake on the wheel which was down. I ended up going sideways on one wheel a tail wheel and wing tip.

Luckily the good tyre held out and the only damage to the aeroplane apart from that done by the bullets, was a wing tip which is easily replaceable. I hopped out and went off to the M.O. to get a lot of metal splinters picked out of my leg and wrist. I felt jolly glad to be down on the ground without having caught fire.

On 7 October, the squadron engaged a large formation of Ju 87s and Me 110s, the latter, as ever, acting as fighter escort, flying over the coast in a north-west path. Eric was flying as Blue 1:

Blue 1 after attacking Ju 88 without noticing results attacked several strings of Me 110s in line astern behind the bombers before they had time to form defensive circles. He got in burst on last E/A of one line and one of its engines streamed glycol. He then attacked single Me 110, the crew baled out and E/A dived vertically into the sea.

For his part in this dogfight, a further 'damaged' was added to Eric's score. The crew of the downed Me 110, an E-1 variant from 4/ZG26 which was coded 3U+FM and had the *werk nummer* 3427, consisted of Oberfeldwebel Erwin Gensler (pilot) and Unteroffizier Franz Hafner (Bordfunker). They were picked up by a RAF Rescue Launch off Ringstead Bay on Dorset's Jurassic Coast.

Eric added a further two enemy aircraft to his tally during the Battle of Britain, these included a Me 109 on 28 November. On that occasion, 152 Squadron was flying at 22,000ft close to the Needles when they were engaged by a large formation of Luftwaffe fighters:

Blue 1 (P/O Marrs) suddenly saw one of them about 100 yards on his right. It slipped across to the left beneath him and dived straight for France. Blue 1 followed it and caught it up at 10,000ft and about 10 miles south of the Needles. He waited his time and closed in to about 100yds. Enemy aircraft was not weaving or turning at all and evidently did not suspect being pursued. Blue 1 gave short burst of

1 sec from astern and slightly underneath. Black smoke came from beneath and oil splattered on his windscreen. Enemy aircraft did a half roll and dived down. Blue 1 broke away and lost sight of it for a short time, and when he looked again the pilot was floating down by parachute and his machine was descending in flames in fragments and had exploded in the air. It was this enemy aircraft that had previously attacked Blue 2 (P/O Watson).

Marrs was forced to return to Warmwell because of the oil on his cockpit windscreen.

On 7 January 1941, Eric was awarded the DFC. He went on to destroy a further two enemy aircraft that year, one in January and another when the squadron moved to RAF Portreath, Cornwall.

On 24 July 1941, the squadron was providing escort cover for Handley Page Hampdens that were on a mission to bomb the warships *Scharnhorst* and *Gneisenau*, in harbour at Brest, France. Heavy flak was encountered over the target area and Eric's aircraft was hit. He was last seen going towards the French coast. His aircraft hit the ground and exploded on impact, killing him instantly.

At the time of Eric's death, Flight Lieutenant Massey was serving with the squadron as a rigger and remembers that tragic day: A sad blow to the Squadron and keenly felt by everyone, being well liked, a good Flight Commander and admired by all. A couple of the pilots were so frustrated on seeing Eric fall out of the sky they broke formation, went down and proceeded to "dig up" every gun position they could find.

Eric was buried in Kerfautras Cemetery, Brest.

MARSH, Sergeant Edward Howard
No.156314

Edward was born on 20 February 1916, at Netherton, Dudley. He was educated at Dudley Grammar School, close to his home in the Midlands.

He joined the RAFVR in July 1939 as an Airman u/t pilot (758002) and flew at 14 E&RFTS, Castle Bromwich, before being called-up for full-time service on 1 September 1939. In October of that year he was posted to ITW St Leonards, and carried out a link trainer course at Derby in December. He was then posted to 22 EFTS, Cambridge, on 12

Above: Sergeant Jerry Marsh. (Courtesy of the Marsh family)

April 1940. After further training at 5 FTS, RAF Sealand, and conversion to Spitfires at 7 OTU, Hawarden, on 18 September, he finally joined 152 Squadron at Warmwell on 28 September 1940.

Edward flew on operational sorties throughout October and November, though he made claims during this period. However, he went on to score a tally of two enemy aircraft destroyed, one 'shared' destroyed and a further 'damaged', all in 1941. It was due to this tally that he was given the nickname of 'Gerry' on the squadron.

On 4 October 1941, Edward was posted to CFS Upavon to attend an instructors' course, after which he was posted to 10 FTS at Tern Hill, 2 FTS at Montrose, and then 3 FTS at Hullavington.

Edward was commissioned in July 1943. He retired from the RAF in 1945, attaining the rank of flight lieutenant, going onto work for Wolverhampton Aviation until 1953.

Edward passed away in 2000. His wife recalled her husband as being 'lovely, full of fun and laughter'.

O'BRIAN, Flight Lieutenant Peter Geoffrey St George No.33329

The son of Air Commodore Geoffrey O'Brian, a Royal Flying Corps pilot and founder member of the Royal Canadian Air Force, Peter was born on 16 September 1917, and was educated at Trinity School, Ontario, Canada. He wanted to follow his father into the RCAF, but, having been persuaded to consider the more established RAF, he was awarded a cadetship to the RAF College Cranwell, where he was awarded the Sword of Honour as the outstanding cadet of his intake.[4] He completed his basic training a year later and received his commission on 18 December 1937.

Peter's first posting was 26 Army Co-operation Squadron, which was based at Catterick in North Yorkshire. As adjutant he gained limited experience flying Lysanders. A motor car accident resulted in him being given a desk-bound job.

He was posted to 13 Group as a sector controller until late July 1940 but his passion was flying and he was keen to get back to an operational squadron. As he was declared medically fit, and there was a pilot shortage in Fighter Command, Peter joined 152 Squadron on 18 August as a replacement pilot with thirty-four hours flying, of which only six were on Spitfires.

Though his total flying hours were very limited, Peter soon became well respected by his fellow pilots, as Pilot Officer Roger Hall explains:

> Pete had made the RAF his career; he was therefore probably more acquainted with the service than anyone else in the squadron. He was of medium size with a small dark moustache. He was fairly typical of those who had joined the RAF through Cranwell – thorough and capable.

Peter's first 'kill' came on 27 August when he was flying as Green 2 with Pilot Officer Walter Beaumont leading the section. They soon engaged a lone He 111 about 15 miles off Portland at 15,000ft. Peter follow his No.1 into the attack, the bomber being sent crashing into the sea in flames. Pilot Officer Walter Beaumont's Spitfire, however, was also damaged and he had to bale-out.

On 17 September, Peter flew as Blue 2 with Sergeant Kenneth Holland as Blue 3 and Pilot Officer 'Boy' Marrs leading the section as Blue 1.

Flight Lieutenant Peter O'Brian in front of a Spitfire. (Courtesy of the O'Brian family)

Above: Pictured outside dispersal are, left to right in the front row, Flight Lieutenant Derek Boitel-Gill, Pilot Officer Graham Cox, P/O Pooch, and Flight Lieutenant Peter O'Brian. Pilot Officer Arthur Watson is the individual standing behind. (Author's Collection)

Flying at 15,000ft over Portland, they were vectored north towards Shepton Mallet at 17,000ft. In the resulting action, which has already been recounted earlier in this book, Pilot Officer Marrs' aircraft was damaged and had to land at RAF Colerne. The other two Spitfires continued the attack:

> concentrating on starboard engine until the engine stopped when smoke almost ceased. Blue 3 then attacked with full deflection concentrating fire below on the right wing of E/A. Final attack was made in cloud from port rear quarter. During last two attacks, no return fire was seen.
>
> Blue 2 and 3 lost the E/A going on southerly course.

Flight Lieutenant Peter O'Brian standing in the cockpit of his Spitfire, UM-R.
(Courtesy of the O'Brian family)

Sergeant Holland's aircraft had to land at Yatesbury airfield due to his aircraft overheating.

E/A took evasive violent action throughout the combat. Diving, side slipping throttling back and doing vertical banked steep turns in alternate directions when attacked. It also endeavoured to climb on one engine. This E/A crashed near Imber.

Peter left the squadron in late September to take command of the newly formed 247 Squadron at RAF Robourgh, Devon, flying the venerable Gloster Gladiator. He was promoted to squadron leader on 1 January 1941 and received the DFC on 2 December the same year. The citation stated:

This officer has commanded the squadron for the past 13 months and has participated in a large number of sorties both by day and night. On one occasion, he participated in one of the longest night flights ever undertaken in a single-seat fighter aircraft during which he displayed good judgment and fine navigational skill. His outstanding qualities as a leader have set an excellent example.

A series of training posts followed and, in the latter part of the war, Peter carried out fighter sweeps over the Brest area of France escorting RAF and USAAF bombers, as well as flying a number of anti-shipping patrols.

On 16 April 1943, he was leading 412 (RCAF) Squadron during an attack on German shipping off the Brest Peninsula when Focke-Wulf Fw 190 fighters engaged them. O'Brian's Spitfire was damaged and he was forced to bale-out over the Channel. He took to his dinghy near the French coast.

During the night he heard the motors of a launch and blew his whistle, which was heard by a patrolling MTB of the Free French Navy. After eight hours in his dinghy he was rescued and returned to Dartmouth, where a flight of his Canadian Spitfires was waiting to escort him the last few miles. Despite his ordeal, he led the wing's next operation.

Peter rested during July 1943 before returning to his former post at HQ 10 Group. He was awarded a Bar to his DFC on 6 August 1943, the announcement including the following: 'This officer has displayed high qualities of leadership, great skill and courage, setting an example which has contributed in a large measure to the high efficiency of the squadron he commands.'

From December 1943 until April 1944 he was a student at RAF Staff College and went on to work at the Joint Planning Staff, London. He was Commanding Officer of RAF Leuchars from August 1953 to October 1955.

Peter was awarded an OBE on 1 January 1954 and appointed ADC to the Queen in 1958. He retired from the RAF on 18 July 1959 attaining the rank of group captain. Of his time on 152 he once stated:

> Certainly I was glad to be there in the squadron. I was an amateur compared with other more experienced colleagues. And I was surprised, as I am sure the others were, when I was posted away to take over 247 Squadron as the CO as a Flight Lieutenant, after being with 152 only just over a month.
>
> My view on the Battle of Britain supports the standard version, but I also would support more recognition of those in other Commands who carried out their operational tasks so well.

O'Brian returned to Canada and became vice-president of a publishing company. He retired in 1982 and he died on April 15 2007.

POSENER, Pilot Officer Frederick Hyam
No.41735

Frederick was born in East London, South Africa, on 11 August 1916, He was educated at both St Andrews College and Selborne College, South Africa, where he was a keen sportsman. His family had strong links to Great Britain, with his father often travelling between the two countries on business.

He joined the RAF on a short service commission in December 1938, completing his training at 3 FTS, South Cerney, before being posted to 152 Squadron in October 1939. On 23 October, while with B Flight, which was on detachment to Sumburgh in the Shetland Islands, Frederick was flying Gloster Gladiator N5701. He overshot the airfield and, landing 100ft off the runway, N5701 spun causing him serious injuries. Due to this incident he did not re-join the squadron until it was at RAF Acklington.

On 20 July 1940, Frederick was flying as Green 3, as 'tail end Charlie' at an altitude of 10,000ft. Without any warning, a number of Me 109s attacked his formation. Frederick reported 'tail' before, having been hit,

Pilot Officer Frederick Posener. (Author's Collection)

Above: In this picture taken at Warmwell are, left to right, Frederick Posener, Edward Hogg, and Walter Beaumont. (Author's Collection)

he was forced to bale-out of his Spitfire, K9880. He landed in the water close to the rear of a convoy at sea below the engagement. It is assumed that Frederick's descent was unobserved by the convoy as no vessel came to his aid. His body was never recovered. He was 23 years old.

Frederick had been shot down by Oberleutnant Gerhard Homuth of 2/JG.27. At the time, Gerhard was the Staffel commander. He would go on to become a high-scoring Luftwaffe fighter pilot, only to be killed in action south of Kromy, Russia, on 2 August 1943.

The squadron ORB is strangely lacking detail of the loss of Frederick, but it would appear that seventeen Me 109s of I./JG27 left Plumetot at

Oberleutnant Gerhard Homuth. (Courtesy of Andy Saunders)

לזכרון נשמות

אחינו בני 'ישראל אנשי החיל מקהלת א'סם לונדון
שמסרו נפשם על קדוש השם בקרב העולמי הראשון והשני
תרע'ד - תרע'ח : תרצ'ט - תש'ה

TO THE SACRED MEMORY OF
THE VOLUNTEERS OF THE EAST LONDON JEWISH COMMUNITY
WHO GAVE THEIR LIVES IN THE FIRST AND SECOND WORLD WARS
1914 – 1918   AND   1939 – 1945.

MORRIS HYMAN MYERS,
16   JULY   1916.
FREDERICK HYAM POSENER,
20   JULY   1940.
HARRY TOYK,
4   APRIL   1942.
ABRAHAM BLOOM,
31   DECEMBER   1942.
MAURICE ISENBERG,
1   AUGUST   1943.
SOLOMON RADOMSKY,
12   DECEMBER   1941.

הב משה חי'ם בר יהודה
טז תמוז תרע'ד
הב חי'ם בר 'עקב
יד אב תש'
הב צבי בר משה יעקב
י'ז ניסן תשב'
הב אברהם בר מא'יר
כג טבת תש'ג
הב משה יצחק בר יהודה לי'ב
כא תמוז תש'ג
הב שלמה בר אפרים
כג כסלו תש'ב

Above: Frederick's name is listed on the memorial in his local synagogue in the East London district of his home country. (Courtesy of Jewish Synagogue SA)

12.46 hours as escort for nine Ju 87s of III./StG2 from Cherbourg-Theville, which undertook an unsuccessful attack on Convoy *Bosom* 30 miles south of Swanage. Three Hurricanes of Blue Section of 238 Squadron, from Middle Wallop, arrived late on the scene and were engaged by the 109s. 'A' Flight from 152 Squadron joined in the fight but lost Frederick in the battle. He is remembered on the memorial in his local synagogue in the East London district of his home country.

REDDINGTON, Sergeant Leslie Arthur Edwin No.742516

Leslie was born on 21 June 1914 and lived with his parents in Coundon, Coventry. He was a keen musician and played the violin, as well as enjoyed many sports including tennis and snooker. He was educated at John Gulson School and attended Coventry Junior Technical College. He undertook an apprenticeship at the Daimler Engineering Company

Sergeant Leslie Reddington. (Courtesy of the Reddington family)

in Coventry. In the evenings, he taught mathematics and technical drawing at his previous college.

Reddington joined the RAFVR in 1938 as an airman u/t pilot and began his training at 9 E&RFTS Ansty, being called-up for full-time service on the outbreak of war. Originally he was posted to Bomber Command to fly Blenheims, but declined saying he did not want the responsibility of other people's lives in his hands, only his own.

He was then accepted for fighter training, which he completed at 7 EFTS Desford, finally moving to 10 FTS Tern Hill to complete his conversion to Spitfires. Leslie was 6ft 4in tall and struggled to fit into a Spitfire cockpit.

In August 1940, he was posted to 152 Squadron and acquired the nickname 'Pils' because of the number of tablets he took to help

LOCAL ROLL OF HONOUR

Sergeant Pilot Leslie Reddington who was reported missing in September last year, has now been reported killed in action. When called to the colours he was in the employ of the Daimler Co., Ltd., where he had served his apprentice ship, and had been in the volunteer reserve of the R.A.F. for some time before the outbreak of war. For several years he was a master at the Technical College evening classes. He was 27 years of age, and leaves a widow and two daughters.

Above: A newspaper cutting detailing Sergeant Reddington's death.
(Courtesy of the Reddington family)

him combat the indigestion he suffered badly from. Flying Officer 'Jumbo' Deanesly remembered Leslie as 'a huge Sergeant pilot with a voice to match'.

On 30 September, Leslie was flying as Green 3 in Spitfire L1072 when the squadron engaged a large formation of Me 110s and Me 109s. During this short-lived dogfight, whoever was 'tail end Charlie' for his section, was shot down. Pilot Officer Dudley Williams, who was flying as Green 1, reported that the last time he saw Green 3 was when Reddington was chasing a lone Me 109 towards the French coast.

Leslie was reported missing: His body was never recovered. On one occasion when home on leave, he had told his family that all he had wanted to do was fly, describing flying as 'a wonderful experience'.

ROBINSON, Sergeant Denis
No.60515

Denis was born on 24 June 1918 at Christchurch, Dorset. His father, Percy, had been an airman in the Royal Flying Corps in the First World War. He was educated at the Stationers Company School, Hornsey, London. He joined the RAFVR in March 1938 as an airman u/t pilot. He moved to 21 E&RFTS Stapleford, followed by 26 E&RFTS, Oxford, and, finally, 22 E&RFTS Cambridge.

On the outbreak of war Denis was called-up for full-time service. In October 1939, he was posted to CFS Upavon to attend an instructors' course. He carried out instructional duties at 14 FTS Kinloss and 6 EFTS Cranfield, and 11 EFTS Perth. He was posted to 152 Squadron on 21 June 1940, when it was still at RAF Acklington.

On 25 July Robinson, flying as Black 2, claimed his first success when he damaged a Me 109, firing a total of 2,750 rounds in the process.

On 8 August, flying Spitfire K9894, he was returning from a sortie with Pilot Officer Beaumont over Swanage, when they were intercepted by a group of Me 109s from II/JG 53. Unfortunately, both Spitfires were out of ammunition. 'We should have known better' said Denis, 'we knew it was vital to keep a good look out at all times but were lulled into false sense of security and had relaxed.'

The enemy aircraft swept down, firing at the Spitfires, which immediately took evasive action – but too late:

> The first thing I felt was the thud of bullets hitting my aircraft and a long line of tracer bullets streaming out ahead of my aircraft. I slammed the stick forward as far as it would go. I could feel the straps biting into my flesh as I entered a vertical dive. I felt fear mounting, sweating with my mouth dry and near panic.

With no ammunition, Denis was pursued by one of the Me 109s, which closed quickly on him:

> I simply had to pull out as the airspeed was nearly off the clock. I had to start looking for the enemy. I turned and climbed at the same time. I opened the throttle to emergency boost. I then noticed wisps of white smoke coming from the nose of my aircraft, suddenly my engine stopped. A bullet had gone through my glycol tank thus

Sergeant Denis Robinson. (Courtesy of the Robinson family)

explaining the white smoke. Wildly, frantically searching for E/A but as often happens not a single plane in sight. The release of tension as I realised my good fortune is something that cannot be described.

Denis knew he had to bale-out, going carefully through the procedure in his mind: 'Release the Sutton Harness, make sure all connections to my flying helmet are free and slide the canopy back. Roll the aircraft until inverted, push the stick forward and out I go.' But Denis managed to steady his glide and he was worried that his aircraft might crash into occupied buildings, so he decided to stay in the Spitfire and find a suitable place to force-land:

> I picked a field near Wareham that looked suitable, slid back the canopy and commenced an approach. At about two hundred feet the boundary loomed up, full flap and a flare out near the ground achieved a creditable touchdown.
>
> The Spit slithered across the grass then suddenly I felt her go up onto her nose. With an almighty crash the canopy slammed shut over my head the cockpit filling full of dirt. The aircraft seemed to be upside down and I was trapped. An awful fear of being burned came to me. I grabbed the canopy with all my might and threw it backwards. To my utter amazement, it shot back, I could now see the aircraft had finished up vertically on its nose in a ditch I had not seen from the air.
>
> To my utter horror, I could not move, then realising that I was still strapped into my Sutton Harness an instant pull and I was free. I stood up and my head jerked back this time it being my flying helmet still attached to my radio and oxygen sockets.
>
> Leaving my helmet in the cockpit I jumped down, surprisingly the Spitfire did not burn. I stood back and took in the scene as locals arrived to assist me and I was taken to the nearest pub where I was filled with whiskey. I had a slight bullet graze on my leg but was otherwise unhurt, the next day I was back on ops again.

On 13 August, flying as part of a squadron scramble, Robinson and his colleagues engaged an estimated thirty to forty Ju 87s with escorting Me 109s and Me 110s at 12,000ft. The squadron attacked in line astern from 14,000ft. Denis attacked a Me 109 from behind, the enemy fighter weaving to get out of range of Denis' guns:

Sergeant Robinson's Spitfire crashed in this field near Wareham, Dorset, on 8 August. (Author's Collection)

Above: Both Bf 109 pilots, Hauptmann Günther von Maltzahn (centre) and Hauptmann Heinz Bretnütz (far right) of II/JG 53 each claimed a Spitfire shot down south of Swanage during the engagement with 152 Squadron. (Courtesy of Andy Saunders)

I followed the Me 109 down … [and] flew up alongside my enemy. I slid my cockpit canopy back and could see him struggling to keep the aircraft under control. He could easily have been any one of the pilots in my squadron – a young man just like me obeying orders and scared to death.

Then suddenly his aircraft went into a vertical dive and exploded on impact. It made me feel sick. I had wanted him to get down safely and to see him wave to me standing by his crashed aircraft.

Of life during the Battle of Britain, Denis remembered well the cry of 'scramble!':

Much time was spent hanging around on readiness waiting for the phone to ring with instructions from Control. When it did, it was to say we may get a warning, such as '100 plus forming up over

Cherbourg'. Then you knew that it would be a Squadron scramble and a big show.

You would just sit and wait; this was the worst time, just waiting. When the phone rang again, the orderly would shout 'Squadron scramble angels 15'.

In an instant, you were on your feet running to your aircraft. You would grab your parachute off the wing, buckling it on as you got into the cockpit. Then you would pull your helmet on which was already attached to the radio and oxygen supply.

Somehow, whilst doing all this, you have started the engine. As you taxi into position for take-off you buckle your safety harness. Taking off was a matter of getting into the wind, keeping a sharp lookout for other aircraft, then full throttle and away you go!

On one occasion he remembered the following with great humour:

I was returning from a sortie with Fathogg leading the section and Walter Beaumont flying on the port side and myself on the starboard. I heard a noise come from my wing and when I looked I saw that I had hit the aerodrome windsock and it got caught in my wing!

I landed and was told to report to Bottle. He gave me a little bit of a telling off and that I was to travel up north the next day to a Maintenance Unit and return in a serviceable aircraft. It was great as I had been stationed at the unit before the war and it was good to see some old friends.

Denis left 152 Squadron on 26 September 1940, having flown more than sixty operational sorties, during which time he was left, in his own words, 'utterly drained and exhausted'. He was posted to 6 FTS Little Rissington, being commissioned on 15 January 1941. Following this he was posted to Canada, to 39 SFTS and 32 SFTS in that order. He was released from the RAF in 1946, having attained the rank of flight lieutenant.

He joined BOAC, having previously been seconded from the RAF, later flying for other civil airlines.

Denis once remarked: 'during the Battle of Britain my view of the value of life changed. My value system had changed and my youth had gone. I was 22 years old – why did I survive … Why did others not?'

Denis Robinson passed away on 28 July 2015.

SHEPLEY, Pilot Officer Douglas Clayton
No.33464

Douglas was born on 14 July 1918, at Carlton-in-Lindrick, the youngest of five brothers. In 1926 he moved with his family to Woodthorpe Hall, Derbyshire. He was educated at Oundle School, where he was a pupil from September 1931 to 1935. After leaving school, he went to work in his father's business.

'Doug' wanted to follow his brother's path into the RAF. So, in January 1938, he entered RAF College Cranwell. On graduation he was commissioned on 1 October 1939, joining 152 Squadron that same month. He married Frances Linscott, a nurse from Sidcup, Kent, in the early summer of 1940.

His first official claim was on 8 August, when he was flying as Black 1 on a patrol at 12,000ft over a convoy that was entering Portland Harbour:

> Black 1 on being attacked at 12,000ft by Me 109s. He climbed to 16,000ft where he encountered 10 Bf 109s. He opened fire at from 50 to 250yds on one Me 109 which had been coming up on his tail and had overshot. When he broke away black smoke was pouring from the E/A, bits were coming off the tail, which had been seriously damaged.

On 11 August, he was part of 'B' Flight, of four aircraft, on a patrol over Portland. Ten miles off Swanage a number of Me 109s were spotted in combat with Hurricanes. Two of the enemy fighters broke away and climbed, with the remaining turning to head for home. The flight broke into two sections, with Blue Section chasing the Me 109s heading for home and Black Section going for the two remaining enemy fighters, which were now above them – Pilot Officer Tim Wildblood was the man flying as Black 2:

> After pursuing them for five minutes they overtook them and Black 1 opened fire at about 200yds range closing into 50yds giving short bursts. The E/A was seen to catch fire and dive vertically into the sea. Black 1 turned and attacked the remaining A/C with the rest of his ammunition then broke away leaving Black 2 to carry out the attack.
>
> Black smoke came from his machine and it dived fast and steadily downwards. Afterwards a Ju 88 was seen about 500ft below and Black 2 dived down and fired off remaining rounds but without any

Pilot Officer Doug Shepley. (Author's Collection)

Above: Pilot Officer Doug Shepley sitting in the dispersal caravan at Warmwell. Note the Spitfire that can be seen through the window. (Courtesy of the Shepley family)

noticeable results. Black section then returned to Warmwell landing at 1110Hrs.

On 12 August, Doug was flying with the rest of the squadron over St Catherine's Point at 15,000ft when he and his No.2 noticed a large formation of approximately fifteen Me 109s, which were preparing to attack the other squadron aircraft. The two men immediately climbed to engage the enemy. Doug's Spitfire K9999 was last seen plunging towards the sea.

The Shepley family lost three out of their five children during the early years of the war, which prompted Douglas' mother, Mrs Emily Shepley, and his wife, to start a fund to buy a Spitfire for the RAF. The following newspaper report, published at the time, detailed this decision:

A mother, who has lost a son and a daughter on war service and whose second son is missing, and the six weeks' bride of the missing

Above left: Pilot Officer Doug Shepley and his bride, Frances Linscott, on their wedding day. (Courtesy of the Shepley family) **Above right Another portrait of Pilot Officer Doug Shepley.** (Author's Collection)

---

man have started a fund to replace the Spitfire in which he was shot down. 'Already there is a donation of a hundred pounds,' the *Daily Mirror* was told last night, 'and it should not be long before there is at least the five thousand pounds necessary to buy a Spitfire'.

The young bride, Mrs Bidy Shepley, heard last week that her twenty-one-year-old husband, Pilot Officer Douglas Clayton Shepley, was reported missing.

She went to her mother-in-law, Mrs E. Shepley, of Woodthorpe Hall, Holmesfield, near Sheffield, who had already lost two children.

Mrs E. Shepley's daughter, Jeanne, was killed in the ill-fated steamer Yorkshire as she was returning to her unit of the F.A.N.Y.S. and her eldest son, Flight Lieutenant George Shepley, was lost when he attacked single-handed a German formation over Dunkirk. He was awarded the D.F.C. posthumously.

Now Douglas, who only six weeks ago married Miss Bidy Linscott, of Sidcup, Kent, is missing.

Above: In this picture, left to right, are John Jones, Doug Shepley, Tim Wildblood and Graham Cox. (Author's Collection)

Below: This group of 152 Squadron personnel is made up of, left to right, Christopher Deanesly, Peter Devitt, Doug Shepley, Tim Wildblood, Graham Cox and an unidentified individual. (Author's Collection)

Friends of Mrs Shepley have already rallied round, and money is pouring in. Mr Shepley is a well-known Sheffield business man.

Through donations, dances, and tea parties the full amount of £5,700 was soon raised. In 1941, Spitfire Mk VB W3649 was named *Shepley Spitfire* and presented to the RAF.

W3649 became the personal aircraft of Group Captain Francis Victor Beamish DSO & Bar DFC AF. Like Douglas, Beamish also crashed into the sea on 28 March 1942. At the controls of *Shepley Spitfire*, Beamish had been leading the Kenley Wing and flying with 485 (NZ) Squadron when he was involved in a combat with German fighters, in which W3649 was damaged.

He requested a vector over the radio and was last seen entering a cloud near Calais. It is presumed that he crashed into the Channel, possibly wounded and perhaps unconscious. Like Douglas, his body was never recovered.

In 1979 a public house was opened at Totley, Yorkshire, named the 'Shepley Spitfire'. It was officially opened by Doug's only surviving brother, Seymour.

Below: A view of Spitfire W3649. (Courtesy of the Shepley family)

SHEPPERD, Sergeant Eric Edmund
No.566529

Eric was born on 18 July 1917 at Binstead on the Isle of Wight. He was educated at Ryde Central School. In his teenage years he became a keen tennis player and was noted within his local area as being a strong field sportsman. His friendliness ensured he became a popular and well respected young man within the community.

Above: Sergeant Eric Shepperd in his flying clothing. (Author's Collection)

On 8 April 1919, Eric's father, Mr J.E. Shepperd, died due to wounds he sustained in the First World War while serving with the Hampshire Regiment. Because of this Eric grew up supporting his mother, Ada, as he was an only child.

Eric joined the RAF in September 1933 as an aircraft apprentice and passed his training in 1936 as a wireless mechanic. He served in Iraq with No.1 Armoured Car Company. During this time, he made friends with John Barker and Ralph Wolton, all three of whom presented themselves for pilot selection and served together in 152 Squadron.

On 3 February, Eric, along with Squadron Leader Shute and Pilot Officer Falkson, was scrambled to intercept a lone He 111. Flying Gloster Gladiators, they successfully brought down the enemy aircraft over Druridge Bay, Northumberland. At this time there was a famous cricket player called Dick Shepperd and Eric acquired the nickname 'Dick'.

On 25 July, Shepperd was part of a squadron scramble, flying as Green 2 with Pilot Officer Wildblood as Green 1. Working in pairs, and flying at 11,000ft over Portland, they intercepted a large body of enemy aircraft:

> Sgt Shepperd, Green 2, was attacked by an Me 109, got into a spin and on recovery attacked a Me 109 onto which he dived closing to 200yds. And firing all his ammunition smoke came from the E/A which steepened its dive and crashed into the sea. Rounds fired: 2,480

On 12 August, Eric was part of a squadron scramble to intercept a large raid of Me 109s and Me 110s. When the squadron arrived, the Spitfires dived on the enemy formation singling out their targets. Eric, flying as White 2 with Pilot Officer Bayles as White 1, shot down two Ju 88s. The first burst into flames, the second also caught fire and crash-landed in Godshill Park, Isle of Wight, at 12.30 hours. Eric fired a total of 2,560 rounds.

Most of Eric's aerial combat took place over his home on the Isle of Wight, and it was not uncommon for Eric to fly low over his house after an engagement to show his mother he was safe.

On 18 August, Eric was flying as Yellow 2 with the rest of the squadron when it intercepted an enemy formation that was attacking radar stations in the Portsmouth area. This included a large body of Ju 87s that was heading towards the coast at 4,000ft:

Above: Sergeant Eric Shepperd pictured at readiness with P/O Pooch.
(Author's Collection)

Yellow 2 opened fire at Ju 87 at close range. He closed to 50yds gave two short bursts at close range while E/A was attempting to take evasive tactics. E/A dived into the sea. Yellow 2 attacked another Ju 87 at close range finished his ammunition and broke away. Yellow 2 saw no apparent damage to this aircraft.

Often Eric would travel home to see his mother as well as spending a lot of time with his fiancée, Eileen Harper, who he had met while taking part his pilot training near Stroud, Gloucester. She would often travel to see him on the Isle of Wight and stay with Eric and his mother.

On 30 September, Eric claimed a Me 110 'damaged' west of Portland. He had been flying as Yellow 3 at the time. The squadron ORB states: 'Sgt Shepperd was attacked by 2 Bf 110, and in return attacked one of them which he hit at close range and damaged.'

On 7 October, 152 Squadron intercepted a large formation of Ju 88s, with escorting Me 110s and Me 109s, flying at 17,000ft in a north-westerly direction. Eric chased after three of the bombers and closed to within 50 yards before opening fire. One of the Ju 88s, an A-1 variant from Kampfgeschwader 51 based at Paris-Orly, panicked and jettisoned its bombload. It began to leak glycol and dropped behind the rest of the formation. At about 400ft it went into a spin and fell in flames. All of its crew successfully baled-out.

With the *werk nummer* 8064 and coded 9K+SN, the bomber crashed at Sydling St Nicholas in Dorset at 16.20 hours. It was flown by Oberleutnant Sigurd Hey, the rest of his crew being Oberleutnant Josef Krell, Leutnant Fritz Bein and Oberfeldwebel Chistian Koenig. All four were taken prisoner.

He had flown twelve missions since the start of the Battle of Britain and later recalled his last sortie:

I was shot down when my Air Wing made a day attack on a factory that made ball bearings at Yeovil. Before reaching the target, my right engine got a radiator hit by a Spitfire so that I could not hold my position in the wing formation and began to hang behind.

When I tried to reach the Channel by one engine three Spitfires came up setting alight

Above: The badge of KG51. (Author's Collection)

KG 51

Above: Sergeant Eric Shepperd. (Author's Collection)

my fuselage tank, thus compelling us to bail out from the burning aircraft.

On the ground, I was received by two veterans of the Home Guard with hunting rifles who brought me by car to the Police station.

During the Battle of Britain, RAF Warmwell had a number of problems with rain and other weather conditions. One such occasion occurred on 18 October, when low cloud covered the whole Dorset coast. An X-raid was plotted in the sector by 10 Group and three aircraft were scrambled to intercept, with Eric flying Spitfire R6607. After exhausting his search, Eric turned for home having lost contact with the other two Spitfires. With weather conditions worsening he contacted control and asked for a course home. He navigated with the aid of key ground features.

It is believed Eric then unclipped his Sutton harness and elevated his cockpit seat to gain a better view out of his aircraft. The reason why is not known, but he crashed into a corpse of trees, the Spitfire striking the ground and then sliding 800 yards before crashing into more trees. The Spitfire exploded on impact.

A witness reported that he was working in the fields with his father when he heard the noise of an aircraft engine, then an 'almighty' bang. He ran to the area of the tress but was held back by his father.

The chief controller for 10 Group was visiting the squadron on the day of the incident and when he heard what had happened to Eric he said that he would personally take action against the controller who had sent Eric into the sky in such weather conditions.

Eric's body was recovered from the wreckage. He was taken home on the Isle of Wight Ferry, on 22 October, his fiancée travelling with him. His coffin was draped with the Union Flag and was placed at the front of the ferry.

He was buried with full military honours in the graveyard of the Church of the Holy Cross in Binstead on Wednesday 23 October 1940. The *Isle of Wight Times* carried this report the following week:

> The villagers of Binstead paid their last tribute to the memory of Sergeant Pilot Edmund Eric Sheppard [*sic*], only son of Mrs. Sheppard, of 3 Chapel-road, at the funeral at the Church of the Holy Cross on Wednesday of last week.
>
> The popularity and respect in which Sergeant Pilot Edmund Eric Sheppard [*sic*] was held by all who knew him was shown both by the large congregation present and the many beautiful wreaths that were placed on the grave. He was killed the previous week in a flying accident after a successful career in the R.A.F. during which time he had shot down four Nazi planes and severely damaged others.
>
> An R.A.F. guard of honour was present and the members of his unit acted as pall-bearers. The Rev. C. Ridley Richardson, an R.A.F. chaplain, assisted the Rev. C. Heald, Rector of Binstead, at the funeral service and read the committal over the grave. A trumpeter sounded the R.A.F. *Last Post* and *Reveille*.

SILVER, Sergeant William Gerald
No.563391

William was born on 15 October 1912, at Twyford Avenue, Portsmouth. He enlisted into the RAF on 17 January 1929, at the age of 17, completing his training as an aircraft apprentice in December 1931. 'Bill', as he preferred to be called, had five postings to various squadrons and units until he applied for pilot training and was successful. He completed his training, being classified as an 'average pilot'.

On 30 December 1936, he was posted to 4 FTS at Abu Sueir, Egypt, remaining there until 22 July 1937. He returned to the UK and was posted to 7 BGS as a staff pilot before, on 17 May 1940, he was posted to 4 Ferry Pilot Pool. After completing conversion to Spitfires, he was posted to 152 Squadron on 16 September as a replacement pilot.

On 25 September he was flying P9463 as Yellow 2 with 'A' Flight on his ninth operational sortie. He was on patrol over the airfield at 15,000ft when it was reported that there were three enemy aircraft heading for Portland. The flight turned and aimed towards this possible target. Moving into a search formation they began searching the skies for these enemy aircraft, as the squadron ORB described:

> Red 1 on looking round saw [a] Me 109 sitting on the tail of Yellow 2. E/A fired at Yellow 2 and burst of smoke was seen to come from his A/C. E/A broke away and dived steeply to south. Red 1 peeled off and dived after him coming within range at 1000ft. Red 1 gave short burst from astern and black smoke appeared from machine which carried on in a steep dive through the cloud. The Me 109s were painted yellow underneath.

Bill's aircraft crashed into the Solent off the Hampshire coast just before midday. Eric Marrs wrote a letter to Silver's father, which was published in *The Aeroplane* on 21 September 1945,[5] in which he stated that Silver's Spitfire 'dived vertically into the sea, having been jumped by a 109'. Marrs added that the incident 'shows how careful one must be to watch one's tail'.

Bill's body was washed up near his home at Portchester Castle, Portsmouth. It is believed he was found by his brother, who heard that Bill had crashed into the Solent and went looking for him.

His good friend at 152 Squadron was Sergeant Bill Kearsey, the two having met while serving together with BGS units in the late thirties. Bill remembers that day Eric was killed: 'It really shook me when Bill Silver went; he was a much better pilot than I was.'

Mrs D. Kearsey once noted: 'When someone you knew was killed it was terrible. When Bill Silver went I just sat on my bed and cried, and I couldn't stop though I'm ashamed to admit. Bill didn't know what to do and all he could think to say was, "If you're like this when Silver goes what will you be like when it's me".'

Bill left behind a wife and a baby daughter.

Above: Sergeant Gerald Silver with his family. (Author's Collection)

SZLAGOWSKI, Sergeant Josef
No.780712

Josef was born in 1914 in the Polish town of Kościerzyna, where his father was the town's stationmaster. At the age of 14 he left school and worked in the local power station, training as an apprentice electrician.

In 1933, at the age of 19, he went to stay with his cousin at the coastal town of Gdynia. He lazed on the beach taking advantage of the sun when he noticed a rotary-engine biplane overhead. It was conducting aerobatics and Josef watched in amazement. It was then he knew he wanted to be a pilot.

On his return home, Josef went to the recruiting office and was accepted for training in the Polish Air Force (PAF). His papers arrived in March 1914 and he was posted to the PAF training school at Torun, almost halfway between his home town and Warsaw. He carried out his training completing a six-week glider course and further training on powered aircraft and requested a posting to a fighter squadron.

He carried out further training at Torun, where he had a lucky escape when a fuel tank of the aircraft he was flying, a Polish PZL, dropped through the undercarriage while he was performing aerobatics. He went on to become an instructor at the Polish Cadet School at Deblin.

On 17 September 1939, following the German invasion, Josef and his mechanic, Johnnie Cieslik, acquired a small aircraft and headed for Romania. They flew for three and half hours before stopping for the night, sleeping in their aircraft. The next morning, they took-off as Russian tanks fired at them, one round piercing the port wing. But they gained height and continued their journey.

As they flew over the border they ran out of fuel and Josef landed the aircraft on an athletics field. With help from the local people, he was given food and fuel and took-off again, eventually reaching the city of Constanza, east of Bucharest on the Black Sea, despite having no maps of the country. He found several other Polish pilots had also made it there.

Many pilots were interned on arriving in Romania, but Josef was taken by the underground movement with fifty other Poles to a farm outside the town where they were hidden. They were disguised as refugees and taken to a nearby port where a boat was loading. Josef bribed his way on to the vessel, which was bound for Beirut. At Beirut, he was placed on another ship heading for Marseilles. From there he went to Lyons to a Polish refugee camp.

Sergeant Josef Szlagowski. (Courtesy of John Willis)

Above: Sergeant Josef in the cockpit of his Spitfire. (Courtesy of Gerry Burke)

Below: Sergeant Josef leaning on the wing of his Spitfire. (Courtesy of Gerry Burke)

Right: Another portrait of Sergeant Josef Szlagowski. (Courtesy of the Szlagowski family)

On 16 February 1940, he was accepted into *l'Armée de l'Air*, the French Air Force. However, on 9 March he took a ship from Cherbourg to England. On arrival, he was bussed to the Isle of Sheppey, where he started his training for the RAF.

He was duly posted to 5 OTU Aston Down, Gloucestershire. It was there that he flew a Spitfire for the first time. 'You sat there in the cockpit,' he recalled, 'and the rhythm of the engine made you happy singing to it: you could fly that aircraft without touching the controls.'

It was on 4 August that Josef joined 234 Squadron at St. Eval. On 4 September, he was credited with his first confirmed 'kill' following a combat over Tangmere. He shot down a Bf 110, and then immediately he saw a Dornier 17 in front of him, which he also shot down.

On 4 October, in action against a large bomber formation over the Dorset coast, he attacked one of the enemy aircraft which then broke in half: He recalled seeing a German airman stranded in the gap between both halves. Josef was close enough to see him stretch his arms up to try and cut something. For what seemed an eternity the man clung to the wreckage before he was thrown free. He was unable to open his parachute as he hurled towards the ground. It was a moment Josef never forgot:

> I thought of trying to rescue him. I thought to myself, 'Oh God, if only I could catch him on a wing and bring him down gently'. I will never forget it. I will always see that fellow coming down without his parachute open.

It is interesting to note that combat reports state he claimed a Me 110 and a Do 17 destroyed on 4 October. However, there are no records of these in the squadron ORB.

On 7 October, while intercepting a raid of Ju 88s and escorting Me 110s, flying as Green 2:

> Green 2 when about to attack bombers saw 3 Me 110s, firing three bursts at close range and broke away. He climbed back into the sun and saw white smoke issuing from both engines of enemy aircraft which was losing height. He attacked again and broke away when 2 Me 110s were on his tail, landing to refuel at Middle Wallop, then returning to Warmwell.

On one occasion, when there was a 'flap' on that German parachutists had landed on the south coast, both Josef and his great friend Klein took-off unofficially to look for the invaders. It was a day that Josef remembered with great sadness, as Klein failed to return:

> We were playing cards when we were scrambled and we all placed drinking glasses on the game and the money which we were betting with I told someone to look after it so we could continue when we returned. Out of the four glasses two did not get tipped up the right way again.
>
> During Christmas dinner at the Squadron I sat in the corner listening to everybody speak English. If only Zig was here what fun we would have. I filled two whisky glasses, one for myself and one for his best friend. I lifted one up and said, 'Cheerio Zig. Merry Christmas.' Then I started to weep.
>
> The station Warrant Officer noticed me sitting on my own so he brought over a large plate of turkey: 'If you don't eat that I don't know what to do with you, now come and have a drink.'

Josef was posted to 152 Squadron at Warmwell on 21 October 1940. A further move, to 303 (Polish) Squadron on 23 February 1941, then based at RAF Northholt, followed.

Josef was awarded the *Krzyż Walecznych* (Cross of Valour) on 1 February that year. After a period with 303 Squadron, he later undertook instructional duties at RAF Newton, having been posted there on 2 February 1942.

He left the Polish Air Force in 1946, having attained the rank of warrant officer. Josef and his wife settled in England, where he worked for Wilkinson Sword. He died in 1993.

TABOR, Sergeant George William
No.754844

George was born at Woodford Bridge, Essex. Little is known about his education and personal life before he joined the RAFVR in late August 1939. Following the outbreak of war he was called-up and completed his training at 12 EFTS and 10 FTS. On 2 September 1940, he was posted to 65 Squadron, which was based at RAF Turnhouse.

On 9 October 1940 George was posted to 152 Squadron along with his friend Pilot Officer Norman Hancock, who remembered:

> George and I trained together in August, and in September we were posted to 65 Squadron, about four weeks later we both went to 152 squadron at Warmwell, we did not really socialise as myself being an officer and him being a sergeant, however we did go to the pictures sometimes together.

On 10 November 1940, George was flying Spitfire N3176 when he landed back at Warmwell after combat with a burst tyre, having been 'shot up' by Me 109s.

At the beginning of 1941, George was posted to 603 (City of Edinburgh) Squadron, having been promoted to flight sergeant. On 23 July 1941, eight Spitfires from 603 Squadron took-off to provide escort cover for six Blenheims flying on a bombing mission to Béthune. George was at the controls of Spitfire Mk Va W3184. A large of number of Me 109s were scrambled and a fierce dogfight ensued. No one saw what happened to George, it

Right: Sergeant George Tabor's headstone. (Courtesy of the CWGC)

being assumed that he fell victim to one of the German pilots. His body was recovered from the crash site and was buried in Longuenesse (St. Omer) Souvenir Cemetery. He was 21 years old.

THOMAS, Flight Lieutenant Frederick Mytton No.37133

Frederick joined the RAF on a short service commission in March 1935. He completed his training at 3 FTS Grantham on 30 March that year, being then posted to 29 Squadron at RAF North Weald. On 10 May 1937, he was posted to Station Flight at Mildenhall and then to 73 Squadron at RAF Digby on 13 September 1937.

He was a keen sportsman and was the RAF officers' featherweight boxing champion in 1936, 1938 and 1939. He was awarded the title of the Imperial Service Champion of 1939.

Frederick joined 152 Squadron at RAF Acklington, being promoted to flight lieutenant on 15 September the same year. In November, he was detached from the squadron with four Gladiators to Sunburgh as OC Fighter Flight, Shetland Isles, carrying out defensive patrols over the North Sea.

He was recalled to 152 Squadron in December taking command of 'B' Flight, then at Warmwell, on 12 August, following the death of Flight Lieutenant Withall the previous day. Dennis Fox-Male recalled that the 'B Flight commander was Flight Lieutenant (Tommy) Thomas a pugnacious looking little man who was a regular and had boxed for the RAF. He was married and left 152 in November 1941 to become a controller.'

Above: Flight Lieutenant Frederick Thomas. (Courtesy of the Thomas family)

On 12 August, Frederick was flying as Blue 1 when he was one

Above: An informal picture of Flight Lieutenant Frederick Thomas taken at RAF Warmwell. (Courtesy of the Thomas family)

of the twelve aircraft that engaged an enemy formation of Ju 88s with escorting Me 109s and Me 110s:

> Green 1 and 2 followed Blue section each attacked different Junkers 88s which they damaged 1. They then did a combined attack on a Junkers 88 which was last seen emitting black smoke, after pieces had fallen off it. 10 Spitfires returned to base between 12,30Hrs and 13.30Hrs.

Frederick was credited with a 'shared' and one 'damaged' in this engagement.

Having been nicknamed 'Tommy', Frederick continued to take part in operational patrols and combat engagements throughout August and September, receiving a further 'probable' Ju 88 on 25 August. On 26 September, flying as Blue 1, he took-off with nine other aircraft to intercept a large raid of Ju 88s with Me 109s as fighter escort. Soon spotting two Ju 88s flying in close formation, Tommy went into the attack firing all his ammunition but not noticing any apparent effects. The next day, however, he was credited with a Me 110 'damaged'.

On 30 September, Tommy was involved in a fierce combat over the Channel with Me 109s and Me 110s, the following description of which is taken from the ORB: 'Blue 1, (F/Lt Thomas) when about to attack Bf 110s after Red and Yellow sections had attacked, was attacked by Me 109, broke away and lost height failing to contact enemy again.'

This was one of Frederick's last operational sorties with the squadron. In November, he was posted to RAF Middle Wallop, a Sector Station in 10 Group. His new job was as a sector controller. However, he still liked to pay an interest in what his old squadron was doing while in the air – when he had the chance he would often try to be the controller who directed the squadron. Indeed, it is recalled that Flight Lieutenant Derek Boitel-Gill said the following to 'A' Flight at dispersal one morning:

> Group might need us in the next hour. Apparently they have hundred plus on the board over Cherbourg Peninsula; they're not coming our way yet, though to be on our toes sort of nonsense. Tommy's controlling.

Frederick was promoted to squadron leader on 1 December 1940. He stayed at RAF Middle Wallop until he was posted to Canada on loan to the RCAF, advising on coastal air defence systems. In 1943 he completed a twin-engine conversion at Grantham and was posted to the Air Ministry, then to India in 1944.

On his return to the UK he went to 12 HQ Group as a wing commander night operations. He continued with many more staff appointments until his retirement from the RAF in 1958.

He died on 18 September 2001.

WARREN, Flying Officer Charles
No.33482

Charles was born on 15 November 1915, at Witham in Essex. He was educated at St Crispin School and the Royal Grammar School, Colchester. He joined the RAF in January 1935 as an aircraft apprentice and carried out his training at No.1 School of Technical Training at RAF Halton, passing-out in December 1937.

In January 1938, he was awarded a cadetship at RAF Cranwell, where he was a keen sportsman representing the college for fencing. The course was shortened due to the outbreak of war and Charles was transferred to the RAFVR as an airman u/t pilot on 7 September 1939, graduating with a permanent commission on 1 October 1939.

Charles was posted to 152 Squadron, then at RAF Acklington, in late 1939. Moving to RAF Warmwell he did not have to wait long before being in combat. On 18 July, flying Spitfire P9640 as Yellow 3, he was helping protect a convoy in mid-Channel:

> Intercepted Do 215, 40 E/A sighted flying west 2000ft, section turned and followed in line astern. Yellow leader was about to attack when Dornier flashed a white signal. Yellow leader moved slightly to port to identify and then gave a burst from almost astern, then warned by Yellow 3 saw 2 Me 109s one each side of him and heard an explosion as his port wing was hit.
>
> He turned and lost A/C using cloud, returned to convoy and remained there until relieved by Green section. Yellow 3 seeing Yellow 1 and Yellow 2 breaking away right and left and no enemy fighters attacked the Do 215 from astern and fired all his ammunition opening at 300 and closing to 150, he saw no return fire but damage to E/A which did a gentle turn into cloud and was lost.

Yellow section landed back at Warmwell at 11.10 hours, with Charles finding several bullet holes in his Spitfire. A month later, on 11 August, flying as part of Blue Section, he took-off at 10.15 hours from RAF Middle Wallop to patrol over Portland. Ten or 15 miles off Swanage, ten Me 109s were sighted in a dogfight with friendly aircraft. On spotting the approaching 152 Squadron Spitfires, the enemy aircraft broke off the action and headed towards France.

Pilot Officer Charles Warren. (Courtesy of the Warren family)

Above: Pilot Officer Charles Warren in front of his Spitfire. (Courtesy of the Warren family)

On return to Warmwell, Charles took-off again to search for Pilot Officer John Jones, who had failed to return. He joined a number of Blenheims from 604 (County of Middlesex) Squadron. They spotted a He 59 on the water 30 miles off Cherbourg recovering downed airmen. As well as protecting the Blenheims from six Me 109s, the 152 Squadron Spitfires also attacked the He 59, successfully destroying it. There is a possibility that Pilot Officer Jones was on board.

On 22 August, flying as part of Blue Section, Warren took-off from Warmwell to locate two Ju 88s that were close to Portland. They located the two aircraft and Charles received a shared 'kill' with Pilot Officer Eric Marrs for one of the pair. This was confirmed by Observer Corps personnel, who reported seeing a Do 17 crash into the sea off Portland, though this was actually the Ju 88.

Above: Pilot Officer Charles Warren pictured at dispersal. (Author's Collection)

Promoted to flying officer on 1 October 1940, Charles was posted to 12 OTU Benson a month later as an instructor, where he mainly taught Polish pilots. In time, Charles was transferred to Bomber Command and went on to fly Wellingtons, carrying out many operational sorties with various British and Commonwealth squadrons. His award of the DFC was gazetted on 10 September:

> Following an arduous operational tour during the Battle of Britain he changed to Bomber Aircraft during which as Flight Commander

displayed considerable skill and courage whilst on operational sorties to some of the most heavily defended objectives. He is a cool and courageous pilot, who by his personal example has sustained the high morale and fighting spirit of the flight.

Charles passed away on 19 October 2005. He was cremated at Slough Crematorium on 2 November, with a full ceremony arranged by the RAF, including a bugler playing the *Last Post*.

WATSON, Pilot Officer Arthur Roy
No.44187

Arthur was born in Nottingham on 30 April 1921. He lived with his parents in the area of Long Eaton. His father was a sales manager. Arthur was educated at Nottingham High School between 1934 and 1939, where his strengths were in sport. He was keen member of the school's Officer Cadet Training Corps, reaching the rank of drum major.

In September 1939, he was accepted for RAF Cranwell as a flight cadet, but the course was suspended due to the outbreak of war. He enlisted into the RAFVR as an u/t pilot in October 1939. After a short course at FTS Cranwell, he was commissioned on 14 July 1940 and joined 152 Squadron the same month.

Pilot Officer Roger Hall joined the squadron two months after Arthur and remembers his first meeting with him:

Above: Pilot Officer Arthur Watson.
(Author's Collection)

Above: Pilot Officer Watson in front of Spitfire R6592, coded UM-V. (Author's Collection)

Below: Pilot Officer Watson standing next to his Spitfire, UM-V. (Author's Collection)

P/O 'Watty' Watson was very young not yet twenty years old. He was very proud of the fact he had already been in action more than once.

The first time I met him he was casting envious glances at my car which, being almost new, did create more than the usual amount of curiosity. He approached me and in a somewhat callous manner, I thought at the time, asked me if he could have it if I were killed before he was. I said 'Of course you can', thinking at the same time how very realistic these people were in their attitude to life and death. Watty, I think, was one of those people who by their very refusal to be taught was fated to die young, especially in such a game as this. He was far too overconfident in his approach to the whole business.

On 22 August, flying as Blue 2, Arthur took off with two other aircraft at 17.17 hours to intercept an enemy formation 10 miles south of Portland. 'Blue 2 attacked Ju 88 10 miles south of Portland,' read the report on this engagement, 'and saw pieces fly off port engine. E/A dived vertically. Blue 2 followed down to 5,000ft and considers that Ju 88 was damaged.' Blue Section landed back at Warmwell at 18.00 hours.

On 15 September, 'Rex', 'Doc' or 'Watty' as he was variously nicknamed, took off as part of Green Section, 'B' Flight. A formation of enemy aircraft was sighted seven miles south-west of Portland. This formation, consisting of thirty He 111s, was flying at 15,000ft and without fighter escort. The Germans bombed Portland and then headed for back to France:

> Green section carried out attack on a straggler from enemy formation. Green 2 then attacked same E/A for 5 seconds burst, saw smoke coming from both engines and undercarriage falling.
>
> Green 2 attacked another straggler at 6,000ft and after 8 seconds burst E/A blew to pieces in the air and fell into the sea about 15 miles S.W. of Swanage.

One of these two He 111s was G1+GS, a P-2 variant of 8/KG55 with the *werk nummer* 2815. Of those onboard, Unteroffizier Paul Schull was killed, while Gefreiter Paul Zornemann was wounded. The aircraft, however, returned to Villacoublay.

Above: Pilot Officer Arthur Watson in his flying clothing. (Author's Collection)

Below: Unteroffizier Fritz Schupp and Gefreiter Karl Nechwatel. (Courtesy of John Vasco and Peter Cornwell)

The other He 111 was G1+AT which, with the *werk nummer* 1586, was from 9/KG55. Three of the crew, Unteroffizier Andreas Janson, Unteroffizier Fritz Keil and Obergefreiter Rudolf Conrad, were killed, while Unteroffizier Heinz Rothen was captured and became a PoW.

On 27 September, Arthur took-off as part of a ten-aircraft scramble at 11.20 hours. They were to intercept a formation of forty Ju 88s with fighter escort consisting of Me 110s and Me 109s. The squadron attacked the enemy aircraft over Bristol and soon a fierce dogfight ensued. In this, flying as Blue 2, Watty destroyed a Ju 88, which went into the sea 5 miles off the Isle of Wight. He also shot down a Me 110, which crashed to the south-west of Poole. The latter was 3U+DS of 8/ZG26, a C-4 variant with the *werk nummer* 3290, crewed by Unteroffizier Fritz Schupp and Gefreiter Karl Nechwatel, both of whom became PoWs.

During this combat Arthur was injured, having been hit by return fire from two Me 109s over Southampton. He managed to force-land his aircraft and was taken to the local hospital, where he was treated for metal fragments in his arm. Due to his injury he was given a month's sick

Above: Unteroffizier Fritz Schupp pictured in the cockpit of his Bf 110. (Courtesy of John Vasco and Peter Cornwell)

Below: Sergeant J. Lewis, No.5 Battery, 2nd Searchlight Regiment, beside the Me 110 shot down by Watson, and which crashed at Salters Wood near Kimmeridge. Copies of the picture were handed out to the residents of Kimmeridge. (Author's Collection)

Above: A trio of 152 Squadron pilots who are, from left to right, Dudley Williams, Arthur Watson and 'Boy' Marrs. (Author's Collection)

leave. During his time at home he visited his former school, Nottingham High School, from whose records the following is taken: 'He visited the School while on sick leave, and on one occasion gave an informal talk to some of the senior boys.'

Arthur returned to operations in mid-October. He was soon again in combat again, claiming a Me 110 and Ju 88 'destroyed' on 27 November. The Me 110, a C-4 of 8 Staffel ZG26 with the *werk nummer* 3629, was flown by Oberleutnant Artur Niebuhr and Obergefreiter Klaus Theissen. It crashed at Salters Wood, Middle Bere Farm, near Kimmeridge, Dorset, at 11.45 hours. Another pilot involved in this combat was Pilot Officer M.E Staples of 609 (West Riding) Squadron.

Staples disabled both engines of the aircraft which was on an escort mission over Warmwell. Once the aircraft was hit it turned east, looking for somewhere to force-land. But a second attack was carried out by Pilot Officer Watson and, aided by anti-aircraft fire from a nearby battery, the 110 crashed into Salters Wood. Both crew members died in the crash and were buried at St Mary's Churchyard, Wareham, Dorset. They were later re-interred to Cannock Chase, Staffordshire.

On 28 November, again flying as Blue 2, he took-off at 15.51 hours from Warmwell, with nine other aircraft, to meet up with Green Section that was already airborne and on patrol over Bridport. Once together they were re-vectored to patrol at 22,000ft over the Needles, where vapour trails had been sighted. These turned out to be twenty Me 109s.

The Me 109s soon spotted the Spitfires and dived on them. The attacking 109s hit Arthur's aircraft on their first pass. He lost control of his Spitfire and realised he would have to bale-out. Tragedy followed: 'Blue 2, he was attacked from the rear. He was last seen in the air upside down baling out. His parachute appeared to flutter and there seemed to be a gash across it.'

Arthur fell to his death, striking the ground at Middlebere Farm, Dorset. His aircraft crashed nearby. It has been stated that when his body was examined most of his finger nails were missing, a sign that he may have desperately tried to claw open his parachute.

A fellow pilot saw the enemy aircraft attack Arthur and sought revenge. This was Pilot Officer Eric Marrs:

> Blue 1 gave a short burst of 1 sec, from astern and slightly underneath. Black smoke came from beneath and oil splattered. Enemy aircraft did half roll and dived down. The pilot was floating down by parachute and his machine was descending in flames in fragments and had exploded in the air.

Pilot Officer Dennis Fox-Male was also on that sortie:

> Doc, he was slim and dark and tall, about 20 years of age. He had said in his early days that he knew he would not survive the war, but he was a good, though perhaps too dashing pilot and none took him seriously.
>
> It was a shock to learn from one of the pilots that Doc had bailed out but his parachute had failed to open properly and he was killed when he hit the ground. It was a custom in the squadron if you landed safely by parachute to give the Corporal in charge of the parachute packing section the princely sum (in those days) of ten shillings. Our corporal, although he looked rather gormless, had a good reputation and was extremely conscientious. We all admired and thanked him – as we had to.
>
> He was terribly upset at Doc Watson's failure to open his parachute and of course there was an enquiry … We were always instructed to check our parachutes first thing every day. The vital thing was to undo the 'poppers' over the flap which covered and protected the pin in the back of the parachute. When the rip cord was pulled, it jerked the pin out of its metal holder and the parachute unfolded. It was essential to make sure that the pin was straight and not bent.

Above: Oberleutnant Arthur Niebuhr in his car. (Courtesy of John Vasco and Peter Cornwell)

> I was told that Doc's pin was found to be bent right back – as far as you can bend your index finger – and in trying to pull the bent pin out he had in the end ripped the whole patch out – too late for the parachute to open. That evening the squadron was a bit subdued.

Pilot Officer Eric Marrs had another account of how his friend was killed. As he explained it to ground-crew when he landed back at Warmwell, he believed enemy fighters had attacked Arthur from below, firing their cannons with the rounds embedding into the packed parachute, which he would have been sitting on.

Another theory is when his parachute was deploying it snagged on his radio mast and was torn. This radio mast is in the care of the aviation historian and author Andy Saunders and it clearly shows a bent head that could support the theory of this being the cause of his parachute failure.

Watson's death was reported in the *Long Eaton Advertiser* on Friday, 6 December 1940:

The death is announced of Pilot-Officer Arthur Roy Watson, eldest son of Mr. and Mrs. A. Watson, late of College-street, Long Eaton, now residing at 48 Carisbrooke-drive, Nottingham. It is only two months ago that Roy, while battling with a Messerschmitt, was shot in the arm which was rendered useless, and also sustained leg wounds. In spite of his handicap he manipulated his machine with his left arm and managed to land without further mishap. He was in hospital for some weeks, and during convalescence his one desire was again to seek the enemy in air battles.

Above: Pilot Officer Arthur Watson.
(Author's Collection)

He returned to his squadron in due course, and the news of his death last week-end evoked deep sorrow among a wide circle of friends.

Pilot-Officer Watson, who was 19½ years of age, was educated at Long Eaton Secondary School and Nottingham High School. When he left 18 months ago he was successful in passing an examination for the Air Force, it being his intention to take up a permanent commission.

The funeral took place on Wednesday.

WILDBLOOD, Pilot Officer Timothy Seddon
No.33478

Timothy was born on 3 March 1920, the son of Brigadier F.H. Wildblood DSO. He was educated at Colmes Rectory, Alton, from 1926 to 1928, the Towers, Crowthorne, from 1928 to 1933, and Wellington College from 1933 to 1937. He won a king's cadetship and entered RAF College, Cranwell on 1 January 1938. On graduation, he was posted straight to 152 Squadron on its formation on 1 October 1939.

Above: Pilot Officer Timothy Wildblood. (Author's Collection)

Timothy took-off on 27 February 1940 with his friend Pilot Officer John Jones, subsequently being credited with a He 111 'shared', the bomber having crashed into the sea 10 miles off Coquet Island, Northumberland.

On 25 July, flying as Green 1, he took-off with the rest of the squadron to intercept a formation of enemy aircraft flying at between 10,000ft and 11,000ft 20 miles off Portland.

On 8 August, flying as Blue 2, he was on a routine patrol over Portland at 12,000ft when, from above and out of the sun, the flight was attacked by twenty Me 109s. After a brief skirmish the enemy aircraft flew off.

After an hour in the air he and his No1, Flight Lieutenant Derek Boitel-Gill, were preparing to head back to Warmwell when he noticed a lone Me 110 heading towards France being chased by three Hurricanes. The following is taken from the squadron combat report:

He saw a Bf 110 making for France chased by three Hurricanes, their letter being L.Z. He joined in the chase, passed the Hurricanes and fired a short burst at 400 yards on a dive. He then broke off the pursuit when the Hurricanes did so. Rounds fired: 1 burst 400yds.

Tim's first official solo 'kill' occurred on 11 August. Flying as Black 1, he took off from Warmwell with three other aircraft at 10.15 hours to patrol over Portland at 14,000ft. They soon spotted ten Me 109s, which were involved in combat with either Hurricanes or Spitfires from another squadron ten miles off Swanage.

The 109s saw they were outnumbered and two of them broke away and climbed while the rest turned and headed home for France. Tim, being an experienced pilot, knew what the two Me 109s that had climbed were about to do:

Black section sighted the E/A to the right and slightly above preparing to attack the Spitfires so immediately turned and climbed up behind and singled out the two Me 109s.

Below: Standing by the dispersal caravan at Warmwell are, left to right, Pilot Officer Sydney Hogg, Flight Lieutenant Frederick Thomas (back), Flight Lieutenant Latham Withall and Pilot Officer Tim Wildblood. (Author's Collection)

After pursuing them for five minutes they overtook them and Black 1 opened fire at about 200yds range closing into 80yds giving short bursts. The E/A was seen to catch fire and dived vertically into the sea. Black 1 turned and attacked the remaining A/C with the rest of his ammunition then broke away leaving Black 2 to carry on the attack. Black smoke came from this machine and it dived fast and steadily downwards.

Black section then returned to Warmwell landing at 1110Hrs.

It was during this engagement that he lost one of his close friends when Pilot Officer John Jones was shot down and killed. The same thing happened on 12 August when Tim landed back at Warmwell to learn that Pilot Officer Shepley had not returned. Alf Alsop recalls working in the hangar late one evening and encountering Tim:

> I was in the hangar I didn't get to see the pilots that often but Tim Wildblood used to come and see us sometimes. On one visit he told how they'd all chased an '88' and failed to catch him.
>
> Tim was finding it very difficult to cope with the loss of his friends and one evening late August he telephoned Pilot Officer Jones' mother and explained in a state of anxiety/realisation that he didn't have long to survive with the loss of his two closest friends.

With little time to reflect, the very next day Tim was involved in some very fierce fighting, claiming a Me 110 which, according to the squadron ORB, 'went down in an inverted spiral dive', though he did not see it actually crash. On 18 August he claimed a 'shared' Ju 87.

Flying Spitfire R6994, he failed to return from a sortie over the Channel on 25 August. His body was never recovered. He was just 20 years old.

Squadron Leader Peter Devitt wrote to his parents: 'I was always able to rely on him to do a job thoroughly and well, however nasty it may be. He was always cheerful so helped to keep the morale of the squadron during the last few weeks at the very highest standard. He had courage and determination of the highest order.'

On 17 March 1941, he received a posthumous Mention in Despatches for his actions during the Battle of Britain.

WILLIAMS, Pilot Officer William Dudley
No.78985

William was born on 15 April 1915 in East Grinstead, Sussex. He was educated at Bowden House, and Chillon College, Switzerland.

Dudley, as he preferred to be called, joined the RAFVR in April 1938 as airman u/t pilot. He was called-up for full-time service on the outbreak of war, joining 152 Squadron at Acklington in early May 1940.

Below: Pilot Officer Dudley Williams. (Courtesy of the Williams family)

Above: Pilot Officer Williams by the nose of his Spitfire. (Author's Collection)

On 13 August, he took-off with ten other aircraft to intercept a raid by an estimated thirty Me 110s. As soon as the enemy was spotted, the Spitfires pounced: 'P/O Williams attacked a Me 110 and was also attacked. He turned on his back and, seeing what he thought was a Me 110 on his tail, continued diving into cloud.' Dudley lost the 110 in the cloud and returned safely to Warmwell.

On 18 August, flying as Blue 2 at 15,000ft over Portsmouth, Dudley and the rest of the squadron was re-vectored to 4,000ft. On descending they observed an enemy formation, consisting of an estimated thirty Ju 87s with fighter support, 4 miles south of the Isle of Wight. The Ju 87s were seen to break off and were preparing to attack the radar stations below.

'Tally Ho!' shouted Boitel-Gill, leading the squadron into an attack from astern. Dudley picked out one of the Ju 87s, and watched as tracer

Above: Pilot Officer Williams by the nose of his Spitfire. (Author's Collection)

rounds from his guns hit the enemy bomber. The Stuka began to swerve downwards towards the sea.

September was a very busy month for 152 Squadron, and especially Dudley who claimed a 'shared' Me 110 with Pilot Officer H.C. Mayers of 609 (West Riding) Squadron on the 25th. The 110 crashed at Well Bottom, Wiltshire, at 12.15 hours.

Williams had attacked with Pilot Officer Mayers at 19,000ft. Coming directly from out of the sun, the two RAF fighters took the German crew completely by surprise. The Spitfire's bullets killed Schumacher and wounded Scherer. The 110's port engine then caught fire and Scherer lost consciousness as two bullets grazed his skull.

Scherer was an experienced pilot having flown in the Luftwaffe since 1935 on Ju 52s and Me 109s. When he regained consciousness he found that his aircraft was just a few hundred feet from the ground.

Above: Feldwebel Walter Scherer can be seen here on the right. To his left is believed to be his engineer.
(Courtesy of Ken Wakefield)

Despite the fact that he was in great pain and that blood from his head wounds was obscuring his vision, he instinctively switched off both engines, regained control of his aircraft and brought it down in a perfectly executed belly-landing on a hillside at Well Bottom.

The following extract is taken from *Luftwaffe Encore* by Kenneth Wakefield:

Thirteen-years-old John Taylor had just left school for his midday lunch break when Walter Scherer's Bf 110 force-landed near Boyton. Later with school finished for the day, he cycled from his home in Fonthill Bishop to see the German fighter. He remembers that it was in a remarkably good condition and from some men that he knew he heard the story of how the German pilot was captured.

The men were timber cutting in Greatridge Wood at the time and they were the first to get to the crash. They could see the pilot moving about in his cockpit and wondered what his intentions might be. While they were debating what to do an army Bren-gun Carrier arrived to solve the problem. The soldiers from the tracked vehicle removed the gunner from the rear cockpit, wrapping him in his parachute for he was clearly dead.

The timber cutters need have no fear about Scherer for he was in no condition to harm them. In addition to his head wounds, he had a fractured skull, a wrenched and badly brushed spine, two crushed ribs and a broken left leg. A broken tooth had cut his mouth, and congealed blood from his head wounds covered his face.

Cuthbert Orde's drawing of Pilot Officer Dudley Williams. (Courtesy of the Williams family)

Above: Another view of Williams by his Spitfire at Warmwell. (Author's Collection)

Scherer was lifted from his aircraft and taken to hospital in Warminster where, he later recalled, he was extraordinarily well treated. His transfer to a military hospital near Shaftesbury a few days later was, as might be expected, a move for the worse, but he was nevertheless well cared for.

After spending three months in hospital he was transferred to a PoW Camp at Oldham in Lancashire and later moved to Canada. He never fully recovered from his injuries and was recommended for repatriation too, but this failed to materialise. The body of Gefreiter Heinz Schumacher was later buried at Salisbury.

Two days later, Dudley was in combat south of Bristol, claiming another Me 110. Having observed large pieces of metal break away from it, the enemy aircraft was soon streaming glycol and it lost height, crashing near Yeovil. The following is taken from the ORB for 30 September, when Dudley was flying as Green 1:

> Green 1 attacked Me 110 which went down and to left. He followed
> it down through the clouds giving long bursts and saw smoke

pouring from both engines. When satisfied that enemy aircraft would crash, he climbed again and attacked another Me110 which had one engine pouring white smoke when Hurricane of 56 Squadron broke away. When ammunition of Green 1 failed both engines were pouring white smoke, Hurricane attacked again and enemy aircraft went down west of Portland.

The 56 Squadron pilot who 'shared' the claim was Flight Sergeant F.W. Higginson.

Dudley was awarded the DFC on 1 January 1941 for his actions during the Battle of Britain. He went on destroy a further Ju 88 on 14 March 1941.

In October 1941, he was posted to 59 OTU Crosby on Eden, as an instructor. He went on to command the famous 121 (Eagle) Squadron from 1 August to 29 September 1942, before being posted away.

Dudley was released from the RAF in 1945 with the rank of squadron leader. He suffered from angina and passed away on 21 March 1976.

WITHALL, Flight Lieutenant Latham Carr
No.39361

Latham was born on 25 May 1911, in the Shire of Toodyay, Western Australia. He was educated at Scotch College, Melbourne. He joined the RAF, on a short service commission in the General Duties Branch, on 21 December 1936.

Latham was posted to 8 FTS Montrose, where he learned to fly Harts and Oxfords. On 7 August 1939, he joined 19 Squadron based at RAF Duxford, flying the then new Spitfire.

On 12 July 1940, he was posted to 152 Squadron, taking command of 'B' Flight. The very next day he claimed a 'damaged' Ju 88, which was flying close to the Dorset coast. The enemy aircraft escaped into cloud, but there was a large amount of oil covering Latham's port wing on landing back at Warmwell, confirming the Junkers had been damaged.

Latham was remembered well by certain members of the squadron, including 'Jumbo' Deanesly:

> He was flight commander of 'B' Flight. Practically all I learned about Spitfires both flying and on the technical side came from Withall and proved to be of tremendous value. I believe Carr Withall was the

Flight Lieutenant Latham Withall at dispersal. (Author's Collection)

son of a member of the then Australian government. He was married while we were at Acklington in 1939. I don't remember his wife's maiden name and the wedding was at her home and not near Acklington. But I do know they had an interest in Germany pre-war brought about Withall's enthusiasm for gliding.

In general I remember him as a non-typical Australian, introverted. But if he'd had the same luck as I did, would have become a very successful pilot.

On 12 August, Latham was leading the squadron as Red 1, with all twelve aircraft taking off from Warmwell to intercept a large enemy formation over St Catherine's Point. The squadron engaged the enemy at 15,000ft.

Latham was seen chasing after a lone Me 109, which was heading south towards France. It is believed that he was 'jumped' by another 109, his aircraft exploding in mid-air. His body was never recovered.

An account of this engagement from Bayles offers a different explanation of Latham's death:

> I was shot down and slightly wounded and while in hospital heard the sad news that Withall had been shot down off the Isle of Wight and not rescued. Very surprisingly he was a non-swimmer. Later, his wife produced twins, both boys I think. He never lived to see them.
>
> I know he got a bullet through his oil cooler and we know he landed on the sea but we could not find him. He called up and told us he got the bullet in his oil cooler before he went down somewhere south of the Isle of Wight.

Latham was flying Spitfire P9456 at the time. He was the most senior member of the squadron to be killed during the Battle of Britain, as well as the fourth Australian entitled to the Clasp to lose his life in the Battle of Britain. He had married in January 1940 and his twin sons were born six weeks after he was killed on 25 September.

WOLTON, Sergeant Ralph
No.45487

Ralph was born on 26 July 1914 at Henley on Thames and was just 1 year-old when his father died in the Great War. Ralph and his brother accompanied their mother to Sussex, where they stayed with her sister.

He was sent to Gordon Boys School, West Working, Surrey, which was set up by the famous General Gordon for boys whose fathers had been killed during the war.

Ralph joined the RAF in July 1932 as an aircraftman, undertaking ground duties. After completing basic training he moved to the Torpedo Development Flight at Gosport, Hampshire, for nine months.

He was then posted to No.1 Electrical and Wireless School at RAF Cranwell and attended a wireless operator's course that lasted fourteen months. On completion, Ralph was posted to 58 Squadron, based at RAF Worthy Down, Wilshire, where he was trained as a wireless operator/air gunner.

After a period with 142 Squadron in Mersa Matruh, he returned to the UK and was posted to 45 Squadron based at RAF Helwan. By this time he had made friends with two other wireless operators, Eric Shepperd

---

Below: Sergeant Ralph Wolton by his Spitfire. (Courtesy of the Wolton family)

and John Barker. All three would join-up for pilot training together and all serve with 152 Squadron during the Battle of Britain.

In September 1938, he and two friends went for pilot selection, going first to 9 E&RFTS, Ansty, then to 10 FTS at Tern Hill. He completed his pilot training in October 1939. Ralph joined 152 Squadron on its reformation at Acklington.

Ralph was in combat on 25 July, flying as part of White Section with Pilot Officer Holmes. They spotted a lone Do 17, and Holmes turned into the attack followed by Ralph: 'The Dornier came into my gunsight and I pressed the firing button. My Spitfire shuddered under the recoil of its armaments: I watched tracer ammunition strike home.' Two other 152 pilots (Deanesly and Hogg, Yellow 1 and 2) also attacked this lone Dornier, which went down near Fleet.

After this attack, Ralph saw a formation of Ju 87s that were about to dive on shipping in the Channel. He made a banking turn and headed towards the target. It did not take long for him to reach the enemy aircraft. He dived on them making the Ju 87s scatter. He kept one in his sights and fired his remaining ammunition. Smoke began to trail from the enemy aircraft: It turned and went into a steep dive. 'The last I saw,' reported Ralph, 'it was still diving towards the English Channel.' The ORB included the following:

> Sgt Wolton and P/O Hogg also attacked a Ju 87 at which they both fired the remainder of their ammunition. Sgt Wolton fired from the rear closing to about 100yds. E/A dived steeply emitting black smoke. (No.110 Searchlight, Portland) reported that a Ju 87 crashed into the sea west of Portland Bill at the time of the combat. Rounds fired: 2,450

Ralph was credited with a 'shared' for both the Dornier and the Stuka. His next engagement was on 13 August, when he was involved in a fierce fight over Portland with Ju 87s and Me 110s. He scanned the sky looking for enemy aircraft coming in to attack him: He then saw a formation of Ju87s attacking shipping below in Lyme Bay. He flew towards the formation as the rear gunners of the Stukas started to fire. Ralph returned the gesture. The Ju 87s scattered to avoid his rounds:

> My diving attack on the Stukas had been fast and as I pulled up the control column back to climb to a greater height my Spitfire

Left: A Cuthbert Orde drawing of Sergeant Ralph Wolton. Orde recalled Wolton sitting for his portrait in 1940: 'It is over a year since I saw Sergeant Wolton, as he was, but I remember very well that the Station Commander put him on the list because, "he has done extremely well already and will do even better if he gets the chance: a particularly good type of sergeant pilot". He was the cheerful sort of chap I enjoy drawing, though the number of gadgets on his arm made me work overtime! In one respect he is, I think, unique. He baled out into the sea without opening his parachute; he didn't have time! His aircraft had been badly shot up, and his engine was useless; he tried to glide to shore, but with three miles to go his controls, which had been badly frayed, broke. He was low down at the time, but was determined not to plunge into the sea inside the aeroplane, so jumped out and hit the water at, I suppose, a hundred and fifty miles an hour. He wasn't in the least hurt and swam, supported by his Mae West, two miles to a buoy, whence he was in due course rescued. A fortnight later he had to bale out again, this time from over twenty thousand feet. He'd forgotten to do up his belt and had opened his "hood", the sliding cockpit cover, for a moment. Suddenly, having to go into a dive, he shot out of the aeroplane – to his intense surprise. Being a bit short in the arms, he couldn't get hold of the release handle of the parachute, and it wasn't till he was down to a thousand feet that he got it open. I remember his standing me a whisky-and-soda at a Spitfire Ball at Weymouth. He thought it was due to me after drawing his many "trade-marks".' Injuries sustained during these bale-outs left Wolton with a life-long limp. (Courtesy of the Wolton family)

Right: Sergeant Ralph Wolton travelling on a motorcycle along the South Coast near Rottingdean. Note how the headlight has a shutter fitted to comply with blackout regulations. (Courtesy of Peggy Wolton)

suddenly vibrated. There followed two explosions and gaping holes appeared in the wings.

The cockpit filled with smoke and fumes. Ralph slid back his hood and turned off the engine. He could see the coast so decided to glide towards it. Suddenly the aircraft dropped in height and began a vertical dive. Though he was too low for his parachute to deploy effectively, he had no choice but to bale-out. He hit the water hard and was knocked unconscious:

> The next thing I recalled was regaining consciousness and being unable to breathe, everything around was dark green, freezing. I managed to control my fear and held my breath and swam towards the lighter water above.
>
> I broke the surface gasping for air and coughing. I had released my parachute harness, my lungs ached and I felt deeply sick. I managed to inflate my Mae West with difficulty and release the bag of florazine which turned the water around me to a bright green colour.
>
> My legs were beginning to go much numb; my ankle has sustained an injury this being the cause of my pain. I thought I may be able to swim to Chesil Beach, but closer was a target buoy used for the nearby bombing range. I swam to it and with great difficulty got up onto it. I realised that my shoes, wristwatch, and flying helmet were missing.
>
> As I lay there, I heard engines coming towards me, and a RAF Rescue launch pulled alongside. I was taken onto the vessel and received first aid for my ankle. I was taken to hospital where I spent two weeks recovering.

Having recovered, Ralph was soon back in combat. On 26 September he flew as Red 2, with Flight Lieutenant Derek Boitel-Gill as Red 1 and Pilot Officer Richard Inness as Red 3, as they scrambled to intercept a large formation of approximately thirty Ju 88s and Me 109s over the Isle of Wight.

Red Section went into line astern and attacked the enemy formation from above. After a second attack in conjunction with other 152 Spitfires, three enemy aircraft were seen to drop back with black smoke issuing from them. One crashed on the Isle of Wight and the other two fell into the sea 7 miles offshore. Ralph fired 480 rounds in a five-second burst from a distance of 350 yards.

Sergeant Ralph Wolton, possibly pictured in front of the dispersal hut.
(Courtesy of the Wolton family)

Above: The remains of the Dornier Do 17, which was piloted by Unteroffizier Lengenbrink. Lengenbrink was killed in the crash, while the other two crew members were taken prisoner. (Courtesy of Andy Saunders)

On 11 October, the squadron was on a patrol over Dorchester, with Ralph as 'tail-end charlie'. The squadron dived without warning. Ralph tried to follow, pushing his stick hard down and opening up to full throttle. His aircraft began to vibrate and then there was a crunch as one of his wings began to break away from the main frame.

The squadron had scrambled quickly and Ralph had forgotten to strap himself correctly in the cockpit. He was launched from the aircraft and found himself in mid-air, falling at great speed towards the ground. Worse, he then realised his parachute was not strapped on correctly either. Without panicking, he searched again for his chute, which was wrapped around his arm. Finding the D-ring, he pulled it and his parachute opened.

Ralph landed safely on the lawn of a farmhouse outside Dorchester and from there was taken to hospital for a check-up. He was back at the squadron in a few hours.

It was subsequently discovered that his wing had begun to break away due to an incorrect fitting of the aircraft's radiator. The force of his descent caused the bolts holding the glycol radiator to strip away from the mounting and detach itself from the aircraft, thus causing the starboard wing to break off.

Ralph was later commissioned, going on to instruct at a number of FTSs and OTUs, before flying Beaufighters and Mosquito's with Nos. 417 and 239 squadron. He was released from the RAF in 1948 with the rank of flight lieutenant.

NOTES

[1] Quoted from Chris Goss, *The Luftwaffe Fighters, Battle of Britain* (Grub Street).

[2] Quoted by Kristen Alexander on her blog, *Australia's Few.*

[3] Quoted on the school's website: www.dauntseys.org

[4] Quoted in the *Daily Telegraph*, 19 May 2007.

[5] Quoted here from Geoff Simpson, *A History of the Battle of Britain Fighter Association: Commemorating The Few* (Pen and Sword, 2015).

Appendices

P/O Pooch. (Author's Collection)

Appendix I

'Pilot Officer' Pooch:
The 152 Squadron Mascot

'Pilot Officer' Pooch was a white Staffordshire bull terrier who led a charmed life while living amongst the pilots of 152 Squadron. Indeed, it is said that he had more flying hours than some of 152's younger pilots.

Pooch originally belonged to Flight Lieutenant Ernie McNab, who served with 152 Squadron in 1939. When Ernie was posted back home to Canada he left 'Pilot Officer' Pooch with Flight Lieutenant 'Tommy' Thomas. Soon after McNab departed, Thomas married and, on the big day, he presented 'Pilot Officer' Pooch to his bride as a wedding present. Initially terrified by 'Pilot Officer' Pooch, the new Mrs Thomas soon grew see him as a family pet.

When Thomas was posted to Middle Wallop, Pooch was passed on to Flying Officer Cox, and the two became inseparable. It was not uncommon to see Pooch disappearing to visit his 'lady' companions in the nearby villages and his offspring were often seen around the surrounding areas.

In his memoir, Squadron Leader Peter Devitt recounted an event that occurred in the mess one evening:

> On one occasion, we asked the Chief of Police for Northumberland to dine at one of our guest nights. I went to the door to welcome him on his arrival and at that precise moment our squadron mascot, a large Staffordshire bull terrier, came at speed into the hall from the anti-room chasing a cat.

P/O Pooch wearing a pair of airman's coveralls. (Author's Collection)

Our guest caught the dog, which by now had the cat in its mouth [and was] shaking it vigorously. He bravely held open the dog's mouth and the cat went screeching out of the front door.

Another squadron member who wrote of 'Pilot Officer' Pooch, albeit briefly, was Pilot Officer Roger Hall:

The sun was hot outside and the remainder of the flight were enjoying its heat sitting in deck chairs up against the side of the hut. Cocky was giving his dog Pooch a hip bath in an enamel basin.

Sergeant Bill Kearsey also had fond memories of Pooch:

A close-up of P/O Pooch. (Author's Collection)

Cocky looked after Pooch. He would put a bit of bacon in front of him and say 'Trust Pooch!' And Pooch would sit there obediently goggling at the morsel and Cocky would say grandly to everyone 'Look Pooch is a trust hound!' Then of course 'fetch' and Pooch would leap on the bacon and gobble it up.

During a party they all got tight and painted swastikas on each side of him but the bloke that had given him to us complained so they scrubbed them off and painted on red crosses so that passing 109s wouldn't shoot at him, lovely dog.

One trick Pooch was particularly known for was for someone to cradle their arms and call 'kitty cat', where upon he would go berserk. On one occasion when a squadron photograph was being taken, Pooch was included, taking up his favoured position in the centre of the group.

As the photographer was taking so long to take the picture, someone from the squadron shouted out 'kitty cat'; Pooch duly ran at the photographer, knocking over his tripod and camera, much to everyone else's amusement.

Given a length of rope 'Pilot Officer' Pooch would spend hours disputing possession with anyone who would take over the other end. Given a little encouragement he was even known to move the NAAFI wagon by pulling on a rope tied to it.

Aircraftman First Class Alf Allsopp was a fitter/rigger on the squadron:

P/O Pooch and Acting Station Officer Jill. (Author's Collection)

P/O Pooch sitting next to a visiting army officer at the squadron dispersal.
(Author's Collection)

Dear old Pooch was a menace to the ground crews. He could chew anything: He had a special liking for ropes, tent pegs and tail wheel tyres. He got quite a few flying hours as a puppy.

Pooch could be trouble. The wheel chocks had a length of rope so you could pull them clear. Pooch got one by the rope end and kept pulling the chock along and swinging it across the hangar floor fast. Well, it was dangerous and we got the chock off the rope but he wouldn't let go of the rope.

We had this chain hoist for lifting out engines and Cocky said 'right you bastard' and hitched the rope to the hoist and hauled Pooch into the air. He still wouldn't let go. He just hung there and twenty minutes later he was still hanging on – just a thin trickle of blood coming from between his teeth.

Roger Burns, who was the squadron parachute packer, was very fearful of Pooch. The dog knew this, and often made Roger's life a misery during the latter's visits to dispersal to carry out daily inspection of the parachutes.

When the squadron moved abroad, Pooch was left with a pilot who was recovering from injuries suffered in a flying accident. Each week a paw print would be sent to the squadron to show all was well with their beloved mascot.

Perhaps the last word on this unusual member of 152 Squadron should be left to Air Vice-Marshal James Edgar 'Johnnie' Johnson. He remembered Pooch, particularly the occasion when he caught up with him some years later:

In 1945 I was at Biggin Hill. One night out at our local I was speaking to the landlady about P/O Pooch and his antics. Other people in the pub listened when a WAAF asked what squadron I was from when I remembered Pooch. I replied '152 Squadron'.

Above: Some of 152 Squadron's pilots relaxing at readiness with P/O Pooch. Note the paint marking on his body. (Author's Collection)

P/O Pooch being taught new tricks whilst some of 152 Squadron's pilots relax at readiness. (Author's Collection)

She came back with something which I could not believe: 'Do you know he is still alive and living in this village.'

The next day I went up to the nearby village of Leaves Green to visit my old friend. I went up to the side of this large house and heard children's voices coming from the back garden. I opened the gate leading into the garden and saw old Poochy sitting on the path guarding these children playing. I just cradled my arms and cried 'Kitty cat' and he ran into me hitting me with such force knocking me flat onto my back and licking me to death.

By this time the owner of the house came out and believed that Pooch was really attacking me – but soon realised he was just excited to see me. The lady and her husband were interested in Pooch's life and invited me in to tell them about his eventful life with the squadron. They explained that Pooch had been chasing rabbits one day when he fell down a hole in a nearby quarry injuring himself quite seriously and needing many operations to bring him back to full heath.

I will never forget old Poochy; I still have a picture of him on my fire place to this day.

Below: P/O Pooch relaxing with Flight Sergeant Bowen. (Author's Collection)

Appendix II

Squadron Ground Crew

Though it is often the pilots and aircrew of 'The Few' who are most associated with the events of the Battle of Britain, it was the men and women working behind the scenes, such as a squadron's groundcrew, who also played a vital role in the RAF's victory in the summer of 1940.

One of these individuals was Aircraftsman First Class Alfred 'Alf' Allsopp. Having left his family home in Dublin in 1935, aged 15, he enlisted in the RAF. A three-year apprenticeship at No.1 School of Technical Training, Halton, followed. He duly passed-out as an Aircraftsman First Class. Alf was subsequently stationed at RAF Acklington as a member of 72 Squadron when he was posted to 152 Squadron on the latter's formation. He duly moved with his squadron to RAF Warmwell. He remembers the events of 1940 well:

> When I was posted from 72 Squadron in October 1939 the CO sent a personal message down via the Adjutant explaining my posting was a named one. Not just post a fitter, but post 568357 AC1 A. Allsopp.
>
> When 152 Squadron was first formed at Acklington in 1939, Trenchard came to speak to us. We were all gathered together in a hangar, aircrew in front, groundcrew in rear. He dismissed the aircrew and said, "I'll see you later in the mess". He then ordered us to break ranks and gather round. We then got a "pep" talk basically on the lines of "I've sent them away because <u>you</u> are the squadron, not them. Pilots come and go but it is you who will make the squadron work and without you there won't be one.

Of the events at Warmwell in 1940, Alf goes on to add:

At this time the slow running jet in the Merlins on our Spits didn't work too well. In cold weather the engines would backfire a lot. We even had a couple of fires. There was supposed to be a modification coming through, but Flight Sergeant Bowen said to me and Duggie Brown, "We'll make our own; we'll ream out the jet with an instrument maker's broach". We managed that ok but there was no way to calibrate the flow as we hadn't got a flow meter. But Bowen just said, "You're both Halton brats – make one!

So we did, and it worked well. We had the jets fitted before the mods came through. That was the attitude in those days – if there was a problem you didn't wait.

On occasion the aerodrome was bombed and nine delayed-action bombs were dropped. One landed between our billets and the cookhouse. We had no steel helmets at that time and only slit trenches for protection and the odd air raid shelter.

After the raid the Pioneer Corps dug down to the bomb while we stood around as interested spectators, drinking mugs of tea. Ignorance again! We froze when a pickaxe struck the outer casing; they sandbagged that one and blew it up in situ. The sandbags landed on the billet roofs and hung from the telephone lines.

After the raid I went into the hangar and saw this hole in the concrete floor. Flight Sergeant Bowen walked over sucking his unlit pipe as usual. "What d'y think Allsopp?" To this I said, "I think it came in there", pointing up at a matching hole in the roof.

"D'y think there's something down there then?" I thought there could be. "Hmm," he said, "best leave it alone."

I began dragging two toolboxes out of the hangar, at which point the Engineering Officer, Deveraux, who'd already got himself a good hundred yards away, called out, "That's right Allsopp! Get the equipment clear." Well I had to laugh; one tool box had my tools in it and the other, the model aeroplanes I made to sell to the pilots.

Next morning, we were being marched up to work by Corporal Cooper … Suddenly, I saw the hangar roof open like a flower as the bomb went off. All five of us dived flat. I was the only one hurt as they all landed on me. Our Corporal had dived into a ditch, but it was half full of mud and water and he stood up absolutely plastered. We laughed till we cried.

Above: members of 152 Squadron's ground crew moving Spitfires down to dispersal in the early morning. (Author's Collection)

Below: Ground crew at rest. (Author's Collection)

About that time we clubbed together and bought a car, an EPA Swift, 10hp. I think it was a two-seater, and two behind in a pull-out back, of 1929 vintage. As it was joint ownership we had our names painted over each wheel: Willie's wheel, Doug's wheel, Whally's wheel, Alf's wheel and, of course, at the back spare wheel.

There was a Hart biplane in the corner of the hangar which used 240D fuel, so ok to siphon it out for our car. Driving out of the camp one afternoon we were stopped at the gate and the Sergeant said, "This is the fifth time today this vehicle has been through this gate. I don't know where you find the petrol for it and I don't want to know, but I do need a lift down to the station. We took the hint, "Do jump in Flight – we'll take you there at once!"

Boy Marrs was an exceptional pilot. He once made a magnificent landing on one wheel, balanced the aircraft until it had almost stopped before the wingtip touched the ground. The damage to his 'plane was minimal.

The station entertainment officer was Pilot Officer Arthur Howard, brother of the film star Leslie Howard. With the help of the now famous Frank Muir he got together a concert party; Frank was an RAF photographer in those days. We had a band which boasted it could play the Tommy Dorsey version of the *Song of India* as its signature tune, which was entirely appropriate for the band of the Hyderabad Squadron.

Appendix III

A Night out With the Squadron

With the ever-present threat of injury or death, the life of a RAF fighter pilot during the months of the Battle of Britain was physically and mentally exhausting. It is perhaps unsurprising that as the aircrew fought hard they also often lived hard.

The following is Pilot Officer Roger Hall's account of a night out with the squadron during the summer of 1940:

> We got to the Sunray after five minutes or so. It wasn't far from the aerodrome and was tucked away at the end of a lane leading from the main Weymouth-Wareham road. The Sunray was blacked out and it was pitch dark outside when we switched off our lights.
>
> We groped our way to the door, which Chumley seemed able to find in some distinctive manner. He opened the front door calling, "Switch your radar on Roger", and pulled aside a blanket which had been rigged up to act as a further precaution to prevent light from escaping as the main door was opened.
>
> We got inside to find the others already drinking. Cocky seemed to be in the chair as Chumley and I came in and he called out, "Lost again White Section? Biggies coming up for both of you."
>
> The Sunray was an old pub which was full of atmosphere. The ceilings were low and oak beams ran the entire length of them. In between the beams, the ceiling itself was made of wood of the same colour. It seemed dark at first but there was a liberal amount of lamps, not on the ceiling itself, but on the walls, and these gave a soft light that was distinctly cosy. There were tables of heavy oak

around which were chairs made of barrels, highly polished and containing soft plush cushions. Around the walls ran an almost continuous cushion-covered bench, and the windows, from what I could see of them, for they were heavily curtained, were made of bottle glass and were only translucent.

The serving bar in the middle of the room was round and from it hung a varied assortment of brilliantly-polished copper and brass ornaments. There were roses in copper vases standing on some of the tables and a bowl or two on the bar itself. There were sandwiches beneath glass cases and sausage rolls as well.

The visible atmosphere in the room was cloudy with tobacco smoke which seemed to reach its optimum height a foot or so from the ceiling where it appeared to flatten out and drift in horizontal layers until someone passed through it and then it appeared to follow whoever did so for a moment. There was a wireless somewhere in the room, for I could hear music coming from near where I was standing.

I was by the bar with the others and I finished my third pint of bitter and was talking to Cocky. The night was quite early yet, and Bottle was standing up at the bar with Dimmy, Chumley and Pete; they were all laughing at the top of their voices. A bit further along was Ferdie listening to what might, I think, have been a rather long drawn out story from one of the sergeant pilots, while two others seemed impatiently trying to get him to the point. Ferdie seemed to be quite amused at the process.

There were two of our Polish pilots here too, both non-commissioned and their names were so difficult to pronounce that we simply called them "Zig" and "Zag". They didn't seem to take offence at this abbreviation; they were excellent pilots, both of them.

The wireless now started to play the theme of Tchaikovsky's Swan Lake ballet, and when I'd got my sixth pint I mentally detached myself from the rest for a moment. "Wothcher Roger, mine's a pint of black and tan, have one yourself". I was jolted back to reality by this, which was accompanied by a hearty slap on the back from Ferdie, who had wormed his way across to me.

I had my seventh pint with Ferdie and we both edged closer to the bar where the main body of the squadron seemed to have congregated. It was Cocky who, high spirited and irrepressible as ever, said "Come on boys, we've had this, next stop The Crown". We

A squadron dance underway. Note the squadron adjudant dancing with Mary Williams. (Author's Collection)

picked up our caps and made for the door. "Mind the light," someone shouted as the protective blanket was thrust aside for a moment.

The air outside was cold and it hit me for a brief second like a cold shower while I gathered my wits. Chumley piled into the passenger seat. I was feeling perhaps a little too self-confident after the drinks, but I felt sure I would make it somehow.

We got onto the main road again and Chumley directed us to the Crown in Weymouth. The road was fairly free of traffic and I gave the little car full rein for a while. It was dark and just in front of me there seemed to be an even darker but obscure sort of shape which I found difficulty in identifying for a moment. "For Christ's sake, man," Chumley shouted. Cocky's large Humber had pulled up on the verge and its occupants were busy relieving themselves by the roadside, but one of them were standing in front of the rear light and obscuring it.

We were travelling at not much less than seventy-five mph when Chumley shouted at me – and the Humber was only about thirty yards from us when I recognised it. My slow wittedness only now became evident, but I felt quite confident and in complete control of my faculties as I faced the emergency. I pulled the wheel over to the right, not abruptly but absolutely surely, with calculated pressure to allow me only inches, enough to guide the left mud guard past the Humber's off rear bumper.

At the time I was in full control and thinking how fine and assured were my reactions, how much finer they were now than ever they were when I had had no drink. The sense of complete infallibility and the consequent denial of any risk had overtaken me and the feeling, if anything, became accentuated when the little car had passed Cocky's large Humber, which it did by the barest fraction of an inch, to an accompanying shout of, "Look out, 109s behind" from those who were standing by the verge and otherwise engaged. "No road sense, those boys," Chumley remarked.

The Crown was a quite different sort of place from the Sunray. From the outside it was distinctly unpretentious in appearance, just a flat-sided building flanking the back street down by the harbour. It had four windows, two top and bottom, and a door in the middle. We went in and as I had rather expected, it was an ordinary working man's pub.

There were no furnishings to speak of. The floor was just plain wooden boards and the few tables were round with marble tops and the conventional china ash-trays advertising some type of lager or whisky. The bar occupied the whole of one side of the room and the barman greeted us warmly as we arrived. Chumley ordered two pints of bitter. Apparently, the squadron were well-known and held in high esteem.

The others arrived soon after we got there, and the drinks were on me this time. There was a dartboard in the corner of the room and, not surprisingly, we threw badly. What did it matter how we played I thought, as long as we let off some steam?

When we left The Crown at closing time I was drunk, but we didn't return to the aerodrome. Bottle had some friends in Bournemouth that he'd decided to go. I was too drunk to drive and so was Chumley, who had left The Crown before closing time and taken up his position in the passenger seat of my car where he was fast asleep.

Dimmy, was, so he claimed, more sober than I, so said he would drive my car. I made no protest. I relapsed into the passenger seat and fell asleep as the car gathered speed towards Bournemouth. I woke up as soon as the car came to a standstill, feeling a lot more sober. It was about half-past eleven when we went through the door of this quite large private house.

Bottle's and Cocky's car had already arrived and the occupants had apparently gone inside. The door opened, and a girl greeted us. "I'm Pam, come on in the others are here," she said. Everyone was seated in or on some sort of chair or stool and all had a glass of some sort in their hand. There were two other girls beside Pam.

I was beginning to feel rather tired about this time and I would have been glad to get back to camp, especially as I had to be on dawn readiness again. The atmosphere here didn't seem conducive to any sort of rowdery, like The Crown or The Compass, and the girls didn't somehow seem to fit into the picture. They weren't on the same wave length. It was about two thirty in the morning when we finally left.

We arrived back at the mess just after four o'clock, having stopped off at an all-night cafe for eggs and bacon with coffee. I had to be on readiness at five-thirty and it seemed hardly worthwhile going to bed, so I decided to go straight down to dispersal to find I was the only one there. I had just an hour and a half sleep before I was due to take-off on dawn patrol.

Appendix IV

Combat Claims by 152 Squadron Pilots in The Battle of Britain

Akroyd, Pilot Officer H.J.
Ju 87 damaged,   13 August

Barker, Sergeant J.K.
Me 110 damaged,   13 August
Ju 87 destroyed,   18 August
Me 109 destroyed,   25 August

Bayles, Flying Officer I.N.
Me 110 damaged,   13 August
He 111 destroyed,   25 September
He 111 probable,   25 September
Me 110 damaged,   27 September

Beaumont, Pilot Officer W.
Ju 88 damaged,   12 August
Ju 88 destroyed,   12 August
Me 110 damaged,   13 August
Me 109 destroyed,   16 August
Me 109 destroyed,   16 August
Ju 87 destroyed,   18 August
Ju 87 destroyed,   18 August
Ju 88 destroyed,   22 August
Me 109 destroyed,   25 August
He 111 destroyed,   27 August
Do 215 damaged,   7 September

Boitel-Gill, Flight Lieutenant D.P.A.
Ju 88 destroyed,	12 August
Ju 88 damaged,	12 August
Ju 88 destroyed,	12 August
Ju 87 destroyed,	13 August
Ju 87 destroyed,	13 August
Me 110 destroyed,	13 August
Me 110 destroyed,	13 August
Ju 87 destroyed,	18 August
Ju 88 destroyed,	25 September
Me 109 destroyed,	25 September
Ju 88 destroyed,	26 September
Ju 88 destroyed,	19 October*

Cox, Flying Officer G.J.
Ju 88 destroyed,	12 August
Me 110 damaged,	13 August
Me 109 destroyed,	18 August
Ju 88 destroyed,	21 August
Me 110 destroyed,	27 September
Me 110 damaged,	30 September
Ju 88 destroyed,	7 October
Ju 88 destroyed,	19 October

Deanesly, Flight Lieutenant E.C.
Do 17 damaged,	25 July

Devitt, Squadron Leader P.K.
Me 109 damaged,	25 July
He 111 destroyed,	25 September
He 111 damaged,	30 September
He 111 damaged,	30 September

Hall, Pilot Officer R.M.D.
Me 110 damaged,	27 September
He 111 damaged,	30 September

Hancock, Pilot Officer N.E.
Me 110 destroyed,	28 November

Hogg, Flying Officer E.S.
Me 109 destroyed,   8 August
Ju 88 damaged,   12 August
Ju 88 destroyed,   12 August
Ju 88 destroyed,   23 August

Hogg, Pilot Officer R.M.
Do 17 damaged,   25 July
Ju 87 destroyed,   25 July
Ju 88 destroyed,   12 August
Ju 88 destroyed,   12 August

Holland, Sergeant K.C.
He 111 probable,   15 September
Ju 88 destroyed,   17 September
Ju 88 destroyed,   19 September
He 111 destroyed,   25 September

Holmes, Pilot Officer F.H.
Do 17 destroyed,   25 July
Ju 87 destroyed,   18 August
Ju 88 destroyed,   21 August

Inness, Flying Officer R.F.
Me 109 damaged,   25 July
Me 110 destroyed,   13 August
Ju 88 destroyed,   26 September
Me 109 destroyed,   27 September

Jones, Pilot Officer J.S.B.
Me 109 destroyed,   25 July
Me 109 probable,   25 July

Kearsey, Sergeant A.W.
Me 110 damaged,   30 September
Ju 88 destroyed,   14 November

Klein, Sergeant Z.
Me 110 damaged,   7 October
Me 109 destroyed,   28 November

Marrs, Pilot Officer E.S.

He 111 probable,	16 August
Ju 87 destroyed,	18 August
Do 17 destroyed,	22 August
Me 110 destroyed,	25 August
Ju 88 destroyed,	17 September
Me 110 damaged,	25 September
He 111 damaged,	25 September
He 111 damaged,	25 September
Ju 88 destroyed,	27 September
Me 110 destroyed,	7 October
Me 110 damaged,	7 October
Ju 88 destroyed,	14 November*

O'Brian, Flight Lieutenant P.G. St. G.

He 111 destroyed,	27 August
He 111 probable,	15 September
Ju 88 destroyed,	17 September

Robinson, Sergeant D.N.

Me 109 damaged,	25 July
Me 109 destroyed,	13 August

Shepley, Pilot Officer D.C.

Me 109 damaged,	8 August
Me 109 destroyed,	11 August

Shepperd, Sergeant E.E.

Me 109 destroyed,	25 July
Ju 88 destroyed,	12 August
Ju 88 destroyed,	12 August
Unknown damaged,	13 August
Ju 87 destroyed,	18 August
Me 110 damaged,	30 September
Ju 88 destroyed,	7 October

Szlagowsk, Sergeant J.

Me 110 damaged,	7 October

Thomas, Flight Lieutenant F.M.

Ju 88 damaged,   12 August
Ju 88 destroyed,   12 August
Ju 88 probable,   25 August
Me 110 damaged,   27 September

Warren, Flying Officer C.
Do 17 destroyed,   22 August

Watson, Pilot Officer A.R.
Ju 88 damaged,   22 August
He 111 destroyed,   15 September
He 111 damaged,   15 September
Me 110 destroyed,   27 September
Ju 88 destroyed,   27 September

Wildblood, Pilot Officer T.S.
Me 109 destroyed,   11 August
Me 110 destroyed,   12 August
Ju 87 destroyed,   18 August
Ju 87 destroyed,   18 August

Williams, Pilot Officer W.D.
Me 110 damaged,   13 August
Ju 87 destroyed,   18 August
Me 110 destroyed,   25 September
He 111 damaged,   25 September
Me 109 damaged,   26 September
Me 110 destroyed,   27 September
Me 110 destroyed,   30 September
Me 110 destroyed,   30 September

Withall, Flight Lieutenant L.C.
Ju 88 damaged,   13 July

Wolton, Sergeant R.
Ju 87 destroyed,   25 July
Do 17 destroyed,   25 July
Ju 88 destroyed,   26 September

Appendix V

Spitfire Mk Is Flown by 152 Squadron During The Battle of Britain

K9883	Damaged in combat 20 July
K9840	
K9982	Destroyed in combat 26 September
K9901	Destroyed in combat 25 July
K9999	Destroyed in combat 12 August
L1059	
L1072	Destroyed in combat 30 September
N3039	Destroyed in combat 7 October
N3173	Destroyed in combat 25 September
P9382	
P9391	
P9386	
P9442	
P9427	Destroyed in combat 28 November
P9432	
P9509	
P9543	
P9456	Destroyed in combat 12 August
P9463	Destroyed in combat 25 September
R6607	Destroyed in an accident 1 October
R6763	
R6614	Destroyed in combat 11 August
R6810	Destroyed in combat 25 August
R6889	
R6831	Damaged in combat 27 August
R6964	

R6968
R6694   Destroyed in combat 25 August
R7016   Destroyed in combat 23 September
X4025
X4171
X4247
X4258
X4381
X4550

Appendix VI

Roll of Honour: 152 Squadron Pilots Who Were Killed in the Battle of Britain

Pilot Officer Harold John AKROYD

Shot down during a combat on 7 October 1940 flying N3039. He was severely burnt and died of his wounds in hospital the next day.

Sergeant John Keeth BARKER

Did not return from combat on 4 September 1940 while flying R6909. It was believed he was shot down from return fire from a Do 17 25 miles south of Bognor Regis. His body was washed up the next day on the French coast.

Pilot Officer Walter BEAUMONT

Failed to return from a sortie on 23 September 1940 while at the controls of R7016. Crashed into the sea, cause unknown.

Sergeant John McBean CHRISTIE

Shot down in combat with Me 109s on 26 September 1940 flying K9882. Crashed into the sea off Swanage, Dorset: His body was located by the crew of an air sea rescue launch.

Pilot Officer Richard Malzard HOGG

Shot down in combat with Me 109s on 25 August 1940 flying R6810. Crashed into the sea. His body was never recovered.

Sergeant Kenneth Christopher HOLLAND

Shot down in combat with a He 111 on 25 September flying N3173. Crashed near Church Farm, Woolverton.

Pilot Officer John Sinclair Bucknall JONES
Flying R6614, he was shot down in combat with Me 109s on 11 August 1940. He baled-out over the English Channel. His body washed up on French coast exactly a month later.

Pilot Officer Frederick Hyam POSENER
Shot down in combat with Me 109s of 3/JG 27 on 20 July 1940 whilst flying K9880. He crashed into the Channel off Swanage. His body was never recovered.

Sergeant Zygmunt KLEIN
Flying P9427, Klein was shot down during combat with Me 109s on 28 November 1940. He crashed into the Channel off the Isle of Wight. His body was never recovered.

Sergeant Arthur Leslie Edwin REDDINGTON
Shot down in combat on 30 September 1940 while flying L1072. He crashed into the English Channel off Portland Bill. His body was never recovered.

Pilot Officer Douglas Clayton SHEPLEY
Flying K9999, he was reported missing on 12 August 1940 after an engagement with Me 109s and Ju 88s. He crashed into the sea south of the Isle of Wight. His body was never recovered.

Sergeant Eric Edmund SHEPPERD
Killed in a flying accident due to bad visibility on 18 October 1940 while flying R6607. He crashed near Tadnoll Mill, Dorset.

Sergeant William Gerald SILVER
Failed to return from a sortie on 25 September 1940 while at the controls of P9463. He crashed in the sea off Portsmouth.

Pilot Officer Arthur Roy WATSON
Shot down in combat with Me 109s on 28 November 1940, flying R6597. He baled-out but fell to his death due to parachute failure. His aircraft crashed near Wareham, Dorset.

Pilot Officer Timothy Seddon WILDBLOOD

Shot down in combat on 25 August 1940, flying R6994. He crashed into the Channel. His body was never recovered.

Flight Lieutenant Latham Carr WITHALL

Shot down in combat on 12 August 1940, flying P9456. He crashed into the Channel south of the Isle of Wight. His body was never recovered.

Appendix VII

Roll of Honour: 152 Squadron Pilots
Killed After the Battle of Britain

Squadron Leader Derek Pierre Aumale BOITEL-GILL
Killed in a flying accident on 18 September 1941 while serving as an instructor with 59 Operational Training Unit.

Flight Lieutenant Frederick Henry HOLMES
Killed in combat over Germany on 4 December 1944 while serving with 487 Squadron.

Squadron Leader Peter Harry HUMPHREYS
Killed in a flying accident on 11 November 1947 while serving with 115 Squadron.

Pilot Officer Eric Simcox MARRS
Killed in combat while on escort duties over the French coast on 24 July 1941. He was still serving with 152 Squadron.

Flight Sergeant George William TABOR
Killed in combat over northern France on 23 July 1941 while serving with 603 (City of Edinburgh) Squadron.